Hidden Treasure

GORDON ROSCOE

Hidden Treasure

A story for all who wish to get the best from others

Matador
5 Weir Road
Kibworth Beauchamp
Leicester LE8 0LQ
Tel: 0116 279 2299
Email: books@troubador.co.uk
Web: www.troubador.co.uk/matador

ISBN 1 904744 92 3

Illustrations: Rob Anderson

Typeset in 11pt Stempel Garamond by Troubador Publishing Ltd, Leicester, UK
Printed by TJ International, Padstow, Cornwall

Matador is an imprint of Troubador Publishing

Hidden Treasure

Whenever a group of people gathers
together a great potential is created,
a treasure of immense value.

Contents

Acknowledgements

This is a story about people and I must give thanks to those who involuntarily and unknowingly gave their assistance. Many of the characters who play a part in *Hidden Treasure* owe something to real people and therefore I thank the following who all provided some elements of inspiration as I pieced this story together, they are also acknowledged in the names of the characters (who may or may not bear some resemblance to their namesakes).

Alan Marsh, Alice Roscoe, Barry Mitchinson, David Marsh, Derek Jones, Ed Pratt, Eric Hartley, Freda Jones, Geoffrey Roscoe, Gloria Deacon, Helen Heaton-Reid, Henrik Irwe, Ian Robson, Jack Roscoe, Jackie Brangwyn, Jo-Anne Trotter, John Brooke, Judith Sharod, Julie Roscoe, Sarah Blinkhorne, Sharon Roscoe, Steve Phillip, Tessa Roscoe, Tigger Handford-Rice, Tony Gill.

The Author and
The Blue Water Partnership

Gordon Roscoe is co-founder and a Senior Partner in The Blue Water Partnership.

Gordon graduated with a degree in Law in 1976, and joined the Bowater Corporation as a General Management trainee, commencing his working life in the Paper and Packaging industry. His career has taken him into the Automotive Industry, the Music Industry and latterly the Training Industry. His career to date has seen him working in the U.K., North America, Europe and the Middle East.

Gordon developed an early interest in motivation at work as a young sales manager puzzling over the varied performance of team members. Experience overseas showed that people management challenges were universal, only the local detail changed but never the underlying issues of leadership and motivation.

With much management experience under his belt Gordon entered the world of training and development in 1992. As Operations Director for a medium sized training organisation he observed the successes and failures of various training initiatives and linked them to the shortcomings of traditional approaches to developing managers. In particular the common failure of management theory and training seminars to help managers make meaningful changes in their workplace.

His conclusion was that in many cases we get only a small part of the average persons potential at work and this is a leadership failing; yet, with some subtle changes in style and approach leaders can unlock abilities and attitudes that can drive any organisation to success. The Blue Water Partnership was formed in 2000 to present alternative solutions to the challenge of helping managers develop these essential skills. Blue Water is a steadily growing organisation with a network of experienced leadership coaches throughout the UK and Europe and a clutch of clients who are happy to confirm the impressive success that they have enjoyed through working with The Blue Water Partnership.

www.thebluewater.com

1

Hidden Treasure

I admit that this is an unusual book. For a start it cannot quite make up its mind to be either a novel or a textbook. The second reason is that it does not have a single central character; it has several of them. Its purpose is to open your mind to new ideas, to help you think afresh about human potential, about how it may be revealed and brought to life.

The story asks you to reflect on the dangers of making people faceless. When we treat other humans as another statistic, just another pair of overalls on the shop floor or another body behind a desk, we miss valuable enrichment of our own lives and of theirs. In the context of an organisation, not getting to know our people and not dealing with them as individuals is a fatal flaw. It will inevitably lead to the cracking of that organisation and thence either to its destruction or, at best, its existence as a poor and second rate thing.

I have called this book *Hidden Treasure* because it is about something that frequently remains hidden below the surface and yet is of great value. If we only knew it was there then, with just a little effort and technique, we could bring it to the surface and benefit from its richness. The story you are about to read describes what happens when people gather together and what might happen when people gather together. It's about opportunities for people and organisations to grow and prosper, and it's about a deep frustration experienced when this does not happen. It's about the roots of cynicism and failure and optimism and success.

This story begins by showing you the big picture; what can be gained or lost. It graphically illustrates the outcomes of good and bad management behaviours; it shows their impact on organisations of all kinds and on the wider society that surrounds them.

The chapters that follow introduce a series of people and circumstances whose stories overlap and whose destinies share a single strand. The story moves backward and forward in time and each chapter illustrates one of five essential skills that, when used together, will release the potential of team members.

Once you know the lessons to be learned from these pages it's like wearing a pair of x-ray glasses allowing you to see this hidden resource – and you see it everywhere. But a warning for you! This can be great if you are in a position to influence how a group of people work and deeply frustrating if you cannot. Equipped with this knowledge you also see where Hidden Treasure has been, in the history of broken people and of broken organisations, and mourn its passing. Where the treasure is gone: plundered, squandered, exhausted, irrecoverable – you see only an empty shell that once held riches.

This book makes an optimistic assumption about human beings – that each has great potential. It suggests that something special can happen when these creatures of great potential get together: something very special. But there is a bleak side to this picture. What happens when people are gathered together but their potential is not realised? This has sad and far reaching implications for each individual and for those affected by that individual.

When this potential is realised then remarkable outcomes

are possible which may change almost anything: neighbourhoods, businesses, societies, nations, religions - in fact you could argue that only mother nature herself is a greater power on this earth.

2

Jack's Walk (The Big Picture)

Part 1

The great Mechanism roared. To Jack's ear it sounded defiant.

The air vibrated as the huge hammers were propelled with violent earthy thuds into the dissolving material. This was a mechanical force of immense strength that had always exhilarated those who controlled it and left in awe those who watched this great centrepiece of The Factory preparing the raw materials for another day's work.

Jack looked around at the cavernous space that was the hammering and processing room. He came here first as a boy, twenty five years ago. He hated school but loved his apprentice years in The Factory where he was taught practical things, things he could do with his hands; that was Jack's strength. He learned fast, but then he had good teachers. Every machinist was keen to teach the new lads and he soon took pride, like many of them, in the deft use of a new machine or a great result coaxed from an old one. He loved the atmosphere, the noise of hundreds of machines, the start of each day with the thunderous crashing of The Mechanism, the smells of oil, of hot metal, even of the cleaning fluids. It all seemed like home now, it all seemed quite natural, and for many in The Town it had been the inspirational centre of their lives. Jack never thought of leaving or living anywhere else. He had grown with The Factory, learned to use every piece of machinery in the vast place, taught others as he had been taught. He had risen to the challenges that had come with changing times; new ways and methods, new machines – each bringing a new test to keep everyone on their toes. And for the last 10 years Jack had been one of the tight knit team that were entrusted with the great Mechanism, keeping it moving and working, keeping it alive after all those years hard labour – and so they did, delivering it every day ready, oiled, proud and powerful.

The Factory was not just the place where they came to earn their living. Workmates became second family, and outside in The Town those families became friends, supporting each other, playing, imagining, living and loving. It was a great place to work and those that worked there developed a confidence in themselves and a pride in their community.

The Factory grew The Town. Shops, cinemas, theatres, clubs, pubs; the whole place thrived as The Factory thrived. Creativity blossomed, societies of all manner sprung from the confidence and inspiration that was scattered around The Town like priceless seeds. The community produced fresh and exotic growth in the form of a philosophical society, gardening clubs, dramatic and operatic societies, athletic clubs and an educational association with a year round programme of lectures.

Jack's practiced fingers danced a quickstep across the control panel; a sequence of instructions to decelerate the huge cogs whose terrific mass would permit only a slow and graceful grinding to a halt. But today was different. This was not Jack's routine of the past decade. Had the mechanism had thoughts they would have been: 'Why now Jack? It's too soon, I have hardly started my work and this meagre result will not feed The Factory today. Why are you preventing me from doing what I can do?'

Jack listened to the strange sounds he heard around him - echoes. He was hearing The Mechanism's roar bouncing from the giant walls of these giant rooms – for the first time. Never had he listened to silence in this place. Even in the few hours when the machines were quiet, the hum of generators would normally soften the stillness, but not today. As the pounding began to slow in a predictable rhythm that he knew by heart, it was giving way to an audible emptiness. He flicked the catch on the safety guard, swinging back the mesh door to reveal a set of small tight wheels. They were whirring, humming a descending almost musical scale as they spun their inevitable way to a full stop. Lifting the corner of his clean overall he let it catch in the little steel teeth and immediately it was drawn in and he, like a dancer, turned in a mechanical pirouette as the coat was dragged into the machine. He lifted his arms and stepped forward the coat falling away from him at the moment The Mechanism reached its final stop.

Jack was alone. He was a big broad man standing motionless with his back to the silent Mechanism. They were both motionless. Tears were tracking down his cheeks. His dark thick hair framed a broad face, a face known and respected by many in The Town who would hardly recognise it now. Silence was enveloping a place where silence never was, held back only by the ticking of cooling metal. The Mechanism was stilled. Legs planted apart, Jack's solid frame was motionless, his strong arms by his side, hands in fists, shaking – with sadness, rage, frustration, confusion, fear, anger. Behind him The Mechanism, silenced for the last time; the open guard; the hanging coat.

Jack did not look back. After a yawning moment of indeterminate length, he started to walk; striding forward toward the door, into the daylight, across the car park.

A small group stood on the edge of that car park, behind a row of cones. Just beyond them a crowd had gathered outside the high wrought iron gates that marked the boundary with the road. The members of the small group wore hard hats, two were in suits. One shouted at Jack, 'Put your hat on Jack, health and safety'. A third lifted a camera.

Jack walked. He boiled inside, the tears still came and he would have seen little had he been looking. He heard nothing except the roar of The Mechanism and felt nothing but heat and bitter needles. Jack walked, he tore off his shirt as he passed the gates and flung it on the ground. He strode through the crowd that parted before him, no one dared get in his way, even the policeman standing by knew better than to go beyond a token 'Come on Jack' as the big man swept by. Jack just walked. Through the crowd, down The Factory approach road and passing the school he didn't hear the kids in the playground some a little frightened by the man with no shirt. He saw years of faces in the machine shop, in his head the roar of The Mechanism was accompanied by the clatter and chatter of the smaller machines. Jack walked: past the park, along the high street, the rows of shops, the library with its once grand reading rooms. He stepped into the road, oblivious to anything but the scenes in his head, there was a screech of brakes and a startled face behind a windscreen which he also never saw. Staring strangers; some grinned and pointed, others stood away in case..., most shopkeepers didn't grin but saw Jack's walk as a sadness for their town, which indeed it was.

Jack just walked. As the rain began to fall Jack turned the corner of the street where he lived. Then came the explosion. It was like a dull thump that reverberated in the chest. Jack stopped, just yards from his door. He looked up into the sky and the rain washed his face.

Part 2

It is 31 years later, the day after Jack's death. Jack is sitting on a large white sofa in an eternally white room. Opposite him sits a woman who radiates a warmth of spirit; somehow her presence is reassuring. She is wearing a name badge. It says 'Jo-Anne – Afterlife Mentor'. They are watching a playback of key moments from Jack's life – the frame is frozen at a date 31 years previously when Jack's tearful face is washed clean by the rain.

'You know it wasn't your fault Jack?'

'Yes,' replied Jack, 'I learned that, but it was the powerlessness that was so painful. I would like to understand what happened.'

Jack's life had ended well, in comfort and happiness. But some of those memories still tested him. Why had it gone so wrong at The Factory? How did such a dramatic decline take place?

'No problem Jack,' said Jo-Anne. 'It's my role to help you understand.'

The picture before them dissolved and was replaced by another. This was a young man, not Jack.

'The big picture,' announced Jo-Anne.

The young man was Alan Mars, founder of The Factory. He was in his thirties when he developed a great manufacturing idea. The moving Images before Jack and Jo-Anne told a story. They showed Alan's idea developing: at the start too a small business; the first factory (just a shed really); the simple machines that he built by hand with the help of friends and family; Alan the mature man with a growing business and grateful workers in a time when work was scarce; the growing town (no more than a large village at first but later transformed into a bustling, busy place); a boy growing to a young man, Alan's son David; lucrative exports around the world to countries who had not discovered the processes that made Alan successful; a pride amongst the workers and the townsfolk; a great war that had taken workers and, when it was over, had driven business to a new high; Alan's retirement, wealthy, respected, loved.

The Images faded, replaced by the calming neutrality of the white room.

'Is it coming together Jack?' asked Jo-Anne.

Only now did Jack notice that Jo-Anne seemed to be floating above, rather than sitting on, the chair opposite. There was something about her that made him feel at ease, in fact he had no memory of feeling so deeply relaxed during his entire lifetime.

'It's great to see all that,' replied Jack. 'I've seen old photographs of Alan, but seeing him like this – is it a film?'

'No,' Jo-Anne smiled, 'It's not a film. Everything 'is' and always exists, you just need to know how to view it. All I am doing is showing you what 'is'. Are you ready for some more?'

Jack nodded, a bit dazed by what was happening, it was not quite what he had expected beyond the grave, but for some reason he was feeling very happy.

The Images began again. Now the young son David had taken control of the business: times were changing; new materials and processes were being discovered by competitors; overseas clients were disappearing fast as others caught up with Alan's ideas. David brought his own inspiration to The Factory and created a golden age for the business and all who were associated with it. Jack could see that David did this by allowing the people that worked for

The Factory to reach their full potential and so, for three decades, The Factory remained many steps ahead of its competitors. When a product was enjoying its greatest success, something new was always being developed. Ideas flowed like liquid gold through the organisation seemingly springing from every point, and a great and exciting creativity energised the place. Competitors came and went whilst The Factory thrived. The original products were soon a fond memory as employees learned to change and develop. Constantly they generated change for the better, people at every level in the organisation gaining satisfaction from making things work and then work better. They learned that change was a source of wonderful motivation, not for them the endless drudgery of the same job day after day after month after year. Instead, great innovation meant that everyone was always learning something new, yet no one was frightened of change. David had created a way of working between all employees of The Factory and this 'way' had unlocked incredible resources of talent and energy. David had done what came naturally to him, but even he was stunned by what happened and how happy and productive it made people.

David's 'way' meant that people were encouraged and helped to learn. None doubted their own ability to do new things, they weren't scared to experiment and learn, people were not in fear of criticism. Instead, they knew they could rely on support and so people helped each other. This brought with it a level of productivity that astonished outsiders; it was fuelled by a real enthusiasm and underpinned by a deep sense of satisfaction and achievement that lifted people at work and at home. They went home with a greater confidence and self respect that their work had helped them build. As a result, they were better fathers and mothers, more considerate neighbours and friends, sons and daughters who brought pride to their parents. They came to work not simply to earn a living, but to build their self-esteem.

This was David's time, the famous time of The Factory's greatest successes. Jack broke into a huge smile as he saw himself as a young apprentice on his first day at The Factory and he savoured these returning memories.

The Images showed life outside The Factory, a town that was in full bloom. Great friendships built in The Factory were mirrored amongst the families of the employees. People felt proud and successful, they were achieving things, doing a good job, developing ideas, making things of quality. They weren't all wealthy, but all made a reasonable living and they took home from The Factory a self-belief and sense of worth. This spilled into The Town. Along the high street neat shops creatively offered their wares, an impressive library and reading room had been funded through public subscription matched by contribution from The Factory, there was a thriving theatre, a concert hall, parks, churches – everything became symbols of a collective pride. Visitors to this community felt a buzz of life, a purpose and direction; they found a place comfortably prosperous both financially and morally.

Once more the Images faded.

'Are you getting the big picture?' asked Jo-Anne

'Quite amazing,' replied Jack, 'to see all this. I was told my life might flash before me, but not other people's lives as well!'

' Oh yes,' Jo-Anne smiled. 'You could watch anything from any time if you really wanted to.'

'Anything?'

'Yes, you could see anything that ever happened, although most people get bored once they have understood their own lives. You have a particular question you want to answer, a question that has been with you for a long time. Once you've answered it you will find that this,' she waved her hand at the where the Images had been, 'will lose some attraction.'

'Do you really mean anything from any time?' The prospect of losing interest did not seem remotely realistic to Jack. 'Like great moments from history or what happens to my children?'

'Oh yes, whilst you are in this room we can get the Images to show us any person or event at any place or time, past, present or future.'

' Good grief, is there no privacy?'

'No, none at all. But I assure you, once you've answered your question you will want to look ahead. You will soon feel that studying the Images really no longer seems important. Shall we continue with your big picture?'

Jack sat back scratching his head. Just a short while ago he'd been lying in bed, mortal, drifting off to sleep. Now here he was having an intimate conversation with someone he had just met but who felt like a lifelong friend.

'Try not to be concerned,' said Jo-Anne 'That's what we Afterlife Mentors are here for, to help you make the transition. Now, shall we get on and let you answer your question?'

Jack stretched his legs and settled comfortably into the sofa, try as he might he could not shake off this feeling of great happiness. 'Go on then Jo-Anne, I'm ready for a revelation.'

The Images reappeared.

Jack saw himself as a young man established in The Factory enjoying life; these were the great times. He saw how he had been involved in the redesign of the grinding section, it had taken three years from the first discussions about the change, through the gathering of ideas, designing, testing and re designing, construction of the new machines and training of everyone in how to use them. The whole process had in some way involved hundreds of employees and had been deeply rewarding. There had been a great party to celebrate success; and Jack could see now that the whole exercise was typical of how David got The Factory to run. All his managers supported the workforce. The entire workforce were part of The Factory's team, consulted, involved, full of ideas. Everyone knew what they were doing, where they were heading and what the plans were. All looked forward to the next challenge because they knew that they could be successful and would all help each other through. All of this meant that when things did go wrong, people took it in their stride, learned from mistakes and kept moving forward.

Visitors would come from other factories and walk around trying to work out what The Factory did that was special – they looked closely at the machines, studied the processes and pay structures, and no doubt went away thinking they had got the secret. But few of them ever asked how and why the employees worked together.

The Images kept coming and David grew old. His health deteriorated, he had no children and so came the tragedy. David was forced to consider the future of The Factory and there were many offers to buy it from other organisations. Amongst those one stood out, an organisation that wanted to learn from The Factory's success. BleakCorp guaranteed to maintain the jobs of all employees, they would uphold traditions, they would support the future with worldwide resources, The Factory would continue to move forward under fresh new leadership, and as a bonus they would even build a brand new school for The Town. And so David sold the business and shortly after this his life ended.

Looking from his view point in the white room Jack was

pleased that David did not live to see what happened, but then realised that of course he got the chance to see it all in the Images. Perhaps he chose not to. Jo-Anne said that many choose not to see what happened after their transition.

The Images moved to put the final pieces in Jack's puzzle.

BleakCorp did what they promised. They built the school and no one lost their job, well not at first anyhow. They protected the products and the production methods, but they did not protect 'the way'. For a while business was good, it continued seemingly unaltered. But changes were quietly taking place and they started at the head.

BleakCorp appointed a Chairman to take control of their new acquisition. The Chairman's first actions had been to have a parking space painted out for himself by the main entrance and to get a big car to park in it. He had a smart restaurant built for the senior managers next to and in full view of the big works eatery. It was as if the new man needed to demonstrate that he was the most important person in the place. The way he spoke to people was sometimes harsh, accusing when errors occurred, he demanded explanations and liked to make an example of people who failed to meet his exacting standards. He was rarely seen in the manufacturing areas or by the supervisors and front line managers. Quickly the senior managers who were the interface between the Chairman and the line managers began to change; some tried to protect their teams from this new approach, others adopted the Chairman's style.

Looking at these Images, Jack began to understand the big picture. He could see the change led from the top, the fragmenting of trust and co-operation. He could see how those senior managers set a different example to others and how they began to lose the confidence to involve people in discussion and how they began to lose confidence in themselves. He saw them begin to behave in ways designed to impress the Chairman rather than in ways designed to get the best from those they managed. As the Chairman's influence grew, the senior managers co-operated less with each other and so their departments stopped working together. They gradually ceased to see themselves as one, but instead as independent units meeting budgets and fulfilling their allotted tasks. From this followed a change in attitude of all employees; where trust had been, distrust flourished; where even the meek had offered ideas, now few had the confidence to do so, and as people no longer grew through surmounting day to day challenges they lost energy and began to shrink as individuals and personalities. Some became bored, others bitter.

All this time The Factory was doing well, demand was high and the Chairman was happy. He would go to conferences and give keynote speeches about his success. But The Factory had become like a great tree that had lost its roots; the first storm would blow it over.

For Jack, the big picture was becoming clear. He was beginning to see how the disaster had happened. The Images kept coming, showing that as times changed, markets shrunk, technologies developed, competitors progressed and The Factory began to fall behind. It was all so 'blameless', since no one did anything obviously wrong. Well intentioned Directors and Managers managed performance, wrote reports, introduced new initiatives, but in time all agreed that you cannot forever swim against the tide. Valiant efforts were made to come up with new ideas to turn the business around, managers sat together in think tanks, consultants were engaged, and some small successes were achieved. An occasional bright idea would reverse the fortunes of a small part of the business for a while, but never for long. Increasingly the Directors became frustrated since new initiatives seemed to be resisted.

Making change happen began to feel impossible, and increasingly the conclusion was reached that many of the employees were not of the calibre required to meet the demands of a new age. Recruitment policies were instituted to employ bright young hopefuls and proven executives with track records. Established staff slowly began to leave.

Despite all their best efforts the Directors reluctantly accepted that The Factory's time was passing. They explained that it was operating in a declining market. In time there would no longer be a need for its products. The Chairman, now having received a knighthood for his services to industry, was widely regarded as a great man who had got the best from this dinosaur of a business before expertly tending to it in its decline, acting in the very best interests of employees and community. It was acknowledged that he had no choice than to downsize and the first redundancies, although shocking, were felt to be inevitable. He still went to his conferences, but these days to show his expertise at 'protecting shareholders in an economic downturn'.

Jack, watching these Images in the eternally white room, could see that what had been lost was the great treasure that had always kept the business at the forefront of change; the treasure that had brought success over and over again whilst competitors came and went. This treasure was what lay within the people employed by The Factory, the treasure that David Mars had uncovered and displayed for all to see. All it seemed except BleakCorp and the new Chairman from whom that treasure was well and truly hidden.

Now Jack could see it all, the steady decline, the fate of The Town matched to that of The Factory, the spirit of people diminishing as their feeling of self worth was eroded. The same men and women who had been full of life, turned into poor copies of their former selves. The organisation that had once been alive with energy and prosperity now unrecognisable as the same that had enjoyed such great success. Equally The Town declined and one by one, the societies, the clubs, the initiatives just faded away, and great buildings that had served the community so well began to look tired and neglected. The Directors prepared a respectable demise for The Factory. None could be accused of malpractice and all were convinced that they had done the best that could have been done in the circumstances.

It was a long sad decline until the day came when The Factory was finally to close. Most of the machines had long gone, sold for scrap and only the old anachronism that was The Mechanism remained, it was just too difficult to move and too old to have value or be found a new use. The final act of the departing Directors was to order the demolition of The Factory and so it was that Jack became the last employee making the final close down.

Jack sat back in the sofa, the Images stopped. He closed his eyes and the great mechanism roared. To Jack's ears it sounded defiant. When Jack opened his eyes again, Jo-Anne was standing smiling by a doorway that he had not noticed before.

'Thank you Jo-Anne,' said Jack. 'Now I know what happened, I feel much better. I can see what was so good about The Factory and I can see what happened to make it go so bad.'

'Yes, now you have the big picture Jack,' replied Jo-Anne. 'But remember what happened in The Town afterwards, think about what eventually happened to you. The spirit of The Factory did rise again, didn't it?'

Jack thought for a moment 'Yes it did' he said. Then sitting upright as he was grabbed by a new thought he asked 'I can't have another go can I? Wouldn't it be great to start again knowing all of this stuff?'

Jo-Anne's look told him that it was a silly question and her body language told him that she wanted him to join her.

'Before I leave here there are some other things I would like to see in the Images. My relations, history, the future – there is so much. Will I be able to come back here again?'

'No Jack, once you leave this room you will never be able to return. I understand what you want, but just take a look through here first.'

Jack was uplifted with the happiness he had felt since the moment he found himself in the white room. He stood, happy to co-operate with Jo-Anne and just take a look. He walked forward and she swung open the door. An orange glow filled the room and lit Jack's face. He looked through the doorway and smiled broadly. 'Well I never,' he said, 'who'd have thought it,' and he chuckled as he took Jo-Anne's extended hand and they walked through together, Jack knowing that he would never return.

3

Deep Purple and the Yellow Peril (The First Step)

Part 1

A shrill scream sliced through the afternoon air and exploded like a shell burst in the ear of anyone who happened to be within range. A second followed close behind, accompanied by a barrage of high velocity yells. To the observant onlooker the scene offered a staggering array of emotions and behaviours – violence and kindness, tears and laughter, envy and charity, greed and generosity, anger and sadness; in truth, it would be harder to name emotions and behaviours that were not displayed. This landscape would have intimidated many, but Tessa Thompson had quickly learned to take this world in her stride. Even though she was newly qualified and a recent recruit to the teaching staff she was already quite accustomed to school playground duty.

Tessa was brimming with energy and confidence. She loved her work and she loved the school, a place that had undergone a remarkable change for the better in the twelve months since she had arrived. It had been a hellhole: bad kids, bad teachers, bad school. Back then she never thought she would stay, but now the place was transformed. The only cloud on her horizon was that somehow she just kept getting into trouble. It was not that she didn't work hard or couldn't control the children. In fact to the Head Teacher's experienced eye, Tessa looked like a natural. But events seemed to happen around her. It was Tessa's class who always made the most noise. She would never forget one of her first music classes. Whilst other teachers would coax a tolerable tune from their children, Tessa had hers singing at the tops of their voices and banging assorted percussion at full pelt, eliciting an abrasive visit from the feared Mr Bartlett, Head of Maths, whose class was 'being disturbed by this dreadful racket'. And it was Tessa who brought cream cakes for the staff room on her birthday and left the unfinished box on the chair reserved for Mr Pogson Head of English, with the regrettable result that the nickname Cream Pants had filtered through the entire school and now was firmly attached to the unfortunate Mr Pogson. Whilst other teachers attracted traditionally unflattering nick names: Woodentop, Hitler, Batty, Fatty, the Ugly Sisters – Tessa attracted the nickname 'Tigger' because the kids reckoned she bounced with energy like Winnie the Pooh's friend. Tessa rather liked this and so called her more 'eventful' days Tigger days, and she was rather hoping that today wouldn't be one.

Tessa enjoyed watching the developing characters amongst her pupils; the interplay between them was often fascinating and surprisingly close to adult life. An example was Barry Basket whom Tessa was watching right now. Barry was frequently in trouble and if you watched him you could see that this was almost always of his own doing. He was a threatening boy: you would often see him jabbing a podgy finger in someone's face, demanding his own way. Barry was short, chubby and wore glasses. He had flame red hair and was quick to fling insults. Like most bullies Barry had a gang, made up of weaker characters who were really in the gang to protect themselves against him. What Tessa couldn't see was that today Barry had a plan; he had dreamed up a great practical joke that would make his mates laugh and leave him popular and envied by the whole school. Everyone would get to know who had done it but no one would be able to prove it was him. The gang were going to turn the school fountain purple.

Steady Eddie, one of Barry's gang who liked his chemistry, had stolen something from the chemistry laboratory that he assured Barry would 'do the trick'. The bright purple bottle was larger than Barry had expected, but Eddie said just a few drops would do it. Eddie was on his way, bottle under jacket, to do the deed.

Tessa could also see Pogsy. He was quite the opposite of Barry. Tall and lanky, he seemed so impossibly thin that he looked as if he might snap at any moment. Pogsy, real name Percy Dogsworth, was a quiet boy who lacked confidence. He would rarely speak up and would avoid your gaze. He often gave the impression that he was trying to hide himself, consequently even as a tall boy, he walked with a stoop and would sidle along in a way that made others uncomfortable. No one wanted to be Pogsy's friend, but then no one wanted to be Barry's either, it was just that a few pretended to be for self protection. What Tessa couldn't see was that today Pogsy had brought his pet lizard, Godzilla, to school in his blazer pocket. Godzilla was nine inches long and bright yellow. He was one of the few friends Pogsy had. Pogsy hoped to achieve a little respect amongst his schoolmates by showing Godzilla off.

And here was Jackie Bell, always popular and always reliable. Jackie was unusual in that you knew where you stood with her. She was popular not because she tried to be, but simply because most people liked her. They liked the fact that Jackie told you what she thought and could always be relied on to do what she said. From a teachers view point if she ever did anything wrong, Jackie would tell you exactly what she had done and apologise, which made it particularly difficult to get cross with her. Tessa was interested in the way Jackie got such an impressive performance from the school hockey team, not a team of gifted players but for Jackie they seemed to work so hard that the team was successful beyond its apparent potential.

Watching over the playground Tessa could see that the personalities and behaviours of the children significantly affected the behaviour of others around them. People tried to keep clear of Barry, you could see there were fewer children in whichever part of the playground he was in, and as he moved about, an open space seemed to move with him. When he did talk to others, apart from his 'friends', those others would appear to change their personality, becoming quiet and withdrawn. As Tessa watched she could see how Barry was causing these things to happen around him. Pogsy was also on his own, but amongst the crowd. The other children did not avoid Pogsy they ignored him. Others often became irritated when talking to him, and those that were looking for someone to bully saw an easy target in Pogsy. By contrast, Jackie always seemed to be in the middle of others, whether playing or just talking, and those others seemed to be pleased to be with her. You would usually see more smiling faces around Jackie, which made Tessa think that from Jackie's view point the world must be full of smiling faces whilst from Barry's it must be full of frightened faces. No wonder Barry didn't seem to like many of the others and Jackie seemed to like most people.

Today was a bright, but cool, spring day and the playground was lively. The rappers were in their regular section of the courtyard, with their usual audience. Tessa liked this group and would often stand within earshot. A few had started copying the style of the rappers they heard on the radio or saw on TV, but would contrive their own lines. Others gathered round to listen. This was like a little Speakers' Corner since they often used their words to make statements about things in their lives, chat up those they fancied or cleverly insult those they didn't, and Tessa was constantly impressed by the skill and creativity that went into much of this spoken/sung poetry.

It was typical of Tessa that she couldn't just listen, so on this day she started to do a fun dance to accompany what was going on. 'Hey Tigger' came a voice from the group and almost immediately there were half a dozen doing the Tigger dance. There was some laughter and good chat before Tessa's attention was taken by a young first form girl asking her to come to the far side by the fence where she said a man had scared her. Tessa was swiftly over to the fence and a few of the children described the strange looking man with no shirt who had walked past the school. Tessa took a good look along the road, which ran the length of the playground's mesh fence, but there was no sign of him now. Having satisfied herself that all was well Tessa turned her attention back to the rest of the playground. And as she did so the sight that greeted her rooted her to the spot, her mouth fell open and Tessa, for once, was speechless.

In the short time since Tessa started her dance this is what the Head Teacher had seen from the school door: the few children that copied Tessa's dance were themselves copied by others; in some cases the dance became a little more frenzied as energy stored up whilst sitting in the classroom was released; one of the more energetic dancers slammed into Pogsy just as Pogsy was showing Godzilla to some impressionable first formers; as Pogsy lurched forward in response to the unexpected blow, he loosened his grip on Godzilla who, recognising an opportunity for freedom, leapt from Pogsy's hands and made a run for it slithering an erratic but speedy pathway through the playground; startled, and in some cases terrified, children scattered in all directions as the bright yellow Godzilla made his way to and fro with Pogsy in pursuit.

Steady Eddie was in the process of surreptitiously adding his few drops to the fountain when one of those fleeing Godzilla charged into him, catapulting the entire bottle, with its considerable contents, into the fountain and surrounding pool. At this same moment, Barry had chosen to point his podgy finger at the wrong person. Jim's response was a snarled 'get your finger out of my face Fatso'. In a practised motion Barry turned to his group of followers with a smirk on his face that they all recognised. Little Sid clearly knew what was expected and, reaching up, plucked Barry's spectacles from his face, Barry's motion did not falter as he swung back toward Jim with a clenched fist that clipped the top of Jim's ducking head. Jim grasped Barry's substantial midriff and the two were suddenly spiralling in a full-scale wrestling match.

Meanwhile Godzilla's bid for freedom took a fresh turn in the direction of the struggling duo, who by now were dangerously close to the edge of the rapidly colouring fountain. As Godzilla made his determined reptilian way, fear was giving rise to panic amongst some of the more tender members of the playground community. Consequently two unlikely candidates for troublemakers dashed headfirst, whilst looking back over their shoulders at the advancing yellow peril, into Barry and Jim. This impact was sufficient to send their already ill balanced scrummage teetering over the edge of the low parapet that surrounded the fountain and pool, splashing head first into the now distinctly purple and frothy waters.

Eddie had not envisaged froth. But then he had only

imagined using a few drops of the purple liquid and not the entire bottle. The effect and its speed of development was remarkable; not only had the waters turned a deep purple in just a few seconds but a froth of thick bubbles was growing in intensity before his eyes. The fountain, which was a simple vertical spray achieving about two metres in height, looked like it was covered in purple greenfly as the bubbles boiled along the length of the flowing water, and now some were detaching themselves from the top of the spout and floating merrily across the playground. The pool itself around the base of the fountain had disappeared under a purple foam carpet that, like Godzilla, appeared to be trying to make its own break for freedom. It was spilling over the parapet and creeping across the playground toward the main gates.

The sight that met Tessa's eyes was of two dripping boys, purple from head to foot, standing side by side in the fountain. Above their heads, purple bubbles were floating upward caught by a light breeze, and at their feet encroaching purple foam was spreading toward her. Elsewhere some children were still running in panic as Pogsy made a dramatic diving tackle that brought him to a grazing halt, clutching a wriggling yellow object in his hands at the feet of the Head Teacher, who was standing at the school doorway and calling the words 'Miss Thompson!'

Tessa groaned and raised her eyes to the skies in disbelief. At that moment as if to seal her fate the rain began to fall. Then came the explosion. It was like a dull thump that reverberated in the chest. Everyone stopped, of course today was the day that they were taking The Factory down. Even though she knew just what the sound was, to Tessa's ears it seemed like the deep laughter of a mischievous spirit who for some reason had decided that today would be a First Class Tigger day!

Part 2

Derek James possessed an irreverent sense of humour and as he grew older it got worse.

Derek enjoyed a good laugh; he had reached the conclusion that laughter was critical to a healthy working environment. He was constantly amused to find himself as Head Teacher and frequently gave in to an urge to hold his thumb to his nose and waggle his fingers at the array of portraits of previous Head Teachers that adorned one wall of his office. He usually succumbed to this temptation on having achieved some striven for goal.

This is why, when Derek stepped through the school door for a breath of fresh air, he enjoyed the series of incidents that he witnessed. He saw the group around Barry disperse and one boy heading furtively toward the fountain; he saw the flash of yellow leaping from Pogsy's hands and the fracas that followed as Barry and his assailant began to struggle together. He anticipated the collision of fleeing children and wrestling boys, noted the purpling fountain and the yellow peril hurtling toward him. He was already looking forward to dealing with the inevitable phone call from the irritating Mrs Basket regarding her precious son; to informing her that his colourful fate was entirely of his own making and that the school may consider a claim against her for damage to the fountain. His mirth was barely controlled when the two purple visions arose from the frothing waters, and it was partly to remove himself from the scene that he summoned the speechless Miss Thompson.

Tessa stepped into Derek James's study and was surprised

to hear his laughter. 'You really are a tonic Tessa. You're an excellent teacher with the valuable ability to brighten up the dullest day: sometimes in most unpredictable ways! I thought you needed rescuing from that scene of devastation in the playground.' Then in response to the look of concern on Tessa's face 'Don't worry the rest of the team will sort it out.'

'Aren't you angry, Mr James?' asked Tessa.

'Not at all, it wasn't your fault. There's no serious damage done and it will give everyone something to talk about for weeks. There's nothing like upsetting the status quo to keep everyone on their toes. Come and sit down, it's nice to get a chance to chat with you. Tell me how you are getting along.'

Tessa was relieved and pleasantly surprised. She accepted a seat in the offered armchair and noted with a raised eyebrow the dart with a suction tip affixed to the nose of the portrait of Derek's predecessor. Derek James had become Head Teacher shortly before her own arrival. They shared the experience of both being relatively new to the school. He had always seemed an approachable man but on this occasion she had been expecting a hard time. But since he was offering her the opportunity for a chat there was something that she really wanted to know, and since Tessa was one to grab opportunities she replied to his question with a question of her own.

'I'm really enjoying things here Mr James, it's kind of you to ask, but there's a question I would very much like to ask you.'

'Go ahead Tessa, I hope you feel that you can ask questions in this school?'

'Yes I do, it's just that we are always so busy. My question is a simple one: in my short time here I have seen this school transformed. But I don't know how it has happened, I just know that it has. The teachers are working harder and having a better effect on the children, and the children are more motivated and better disciplined (despite today's excitement!). How have you done it?'

Mr James smiled as he replied 'That's a simple question Tessa, but I'm afraid not a simple answer. It would take a long time to tell you everything and we have just a few minutes till the end of break, but I can tell you how it all started.'

Tessa leaned forward in her chair delighted to get an answer to the question that had intrigued her for many months.

'When I came here,' began Mr James, 'I saw that there was one thing we had to do, before we could do anything else; one thing that would make everything else possible. It was to do with the way our team – teachers, support staff, pupils, cleaners, everyone – were with each other.'

'Were with each other?'

'Yes, the way they behaved with each other. Let me give you some examples of how the staff used to behave. They won't mind me telling you this, they would tell you themselves if you asked them. Take Mr Bartlett, Head of Maths. He was quite frankly an unpleasant man, or that's how he appeared. He was aggressive. By that I mean that people frequently, and in some cases constantly, felt threatened by him. His classroom style was to shout at pupils when he felt unhappy (which was often), humiliating them in front of the class, threatening them with detentions or extra work, taunting them with the prospect of future failure. He ruled by fear, was feared, and as a result was able to squeeze an adequate performance from his classes. Kids did what they had to do to survive in Mr Bartlett's class. At that time it was Mr Bartlett's conclusion that he got the best results possible from poor material. 'The kids in this town are just not very bright,' he would explain.

'But there are lots of bright kids in the school' interrupted Tessa 'in fact I would say that they are all bright in their own way, they all have something to offer.'

'I agree Tessa, but Mr Bartlett's approach blinded him to that truth. His style in the staff room was no different. By the time I arrived at this school the stronger teachers in the Maths department had left, no doubt unwilling to be treated with so little respect, and those that remained were mentally beaten and bruised, disillusioned and lacking in confidence. There was no doubt in my mind that Mr Bartlett had made them like that. They stayed only because they had become such sorry specimens that they could not get jobs elsewhere. I don't think that the words 'fear', 'loathing' and 'hatred' are inappropriate to summarise how most people felt about him.

'As a result the performance of his department in the classroom was a disaster. His sorry crew could not keep discipline amongst the pupils, had little enthusiasm for their work and received no coaching or guidance of any description from Mr Bartlett (although they did get a regular lecture from him, normally focussing on how incompetent they were and instructing them, in the strongest most abusive terms Mr Bartlett could muster, to do better). Alongside his poor view of the quality of kids in the town, Mr Bartlett also bemoaned the quality of teachers, observing that a school with such poor pupils is hardly going to attract decent teachers.'

Tessa's face had flushed with annoyance as she became caught up in what she was hearing. 'So, as a consequence of Mr Bartlett's aggression, children were failing to learn and achieve?'

' Yes Tessa,' replied Mr James, 'they had lost interest and discipline. Mr Bartlett's aggressive style had blighted the entire department, the teachers who taught in it and the pupils who should be taught by it. Unless aware of the true power of aggression, an onlooker might accept that he was doing the best he could with some poor quality people. But with knowledge of the corrosive power of aggression, it was clear to me that this sad situation flowed from just one very influential person. I knew that if we were to improve this school then Mr Bartlett (and anyone else who shared his style) had to be defused.'

Tessa was shaking her head in irritation at what she had heard, but there was more to come.

'In absolute contrast Mr Pogson, Head of English, was dangerous because he lacked courage. Mr Pogson tried hard to be liked by his pupils but instead found himself resented and reviled.'

'As a young teacher he had been full of enthusiasm for developing young minds. He loved his subject, but soon discovered that many young minds were not as keen to be developed as he was to develop them. Mr Pogson's problem arose as soon as others did not do what he asked them to do. Mr Pogson found it difficult to say what he thought when he believed that the other person would not like what he had to say. Either he didn't want them to dislike him or he didn't feel he had the right to speak out – as a result important things frequently went unsaid. The words formed in his head but would not pass his lips, instead those thoughts stayed trapped inside and grew into a frustration that began to eat away at his ambition, his vision and his personality. He began to rot from the inside.

'Visions and ambitions gave way to bitterness and disillusionment. Given time this would take a course toward resigned acquiescence and a timid old age. He was still capable of being kind and helpful, and would respond well and with gratitude to pupils and staff that did as he wished, but to the others he was no more than a spiteful nuisance.'

This contrast to Mr Bartlett had taken Tessa by surprise. She could see how an aggressive person could cause so many problems, but surely what was now being described was much less harmful.

Mr James continued, 'In the classroom he would follow his standard routine, but if a class contained many who were looking for trouble rather than teaching, he would quickly lose control. His passive requests sometimes gave way to futile bursts of anger that did little else than entertain his otherwise bored pupils. Hence baiting Mr Pogson became a game for some. The pupils who wanted to learn got angry with the troublemakers and frustrated with Mr Pogson for not shutting them up. The troublemakers saw Mr Pogson as a soft target and an old fool, and were in no danger whatsoever of being drawn into learning by him.'

'So he was just as much of a problem as Mr Bartlett,' said Tessa as understanding dawned.

'Yes, but that's not all,' replied Mr James, 'his lack of courage in the face of a challenge was darkly balanced by the means he found to vent his frustration. He became a nag, a gossip, a backbiter. No one felt that they knew quite where they stood with Mr Pogson. He would one moment agree with someone about something, and the next be telling another what a fool the first person was. He would promise pupils that he would do things, but often not do them. He was a continued source of dissatisfaction to the staff in his department since he would never tell them bad news (which they usually received in the form of rumour from elsewhere), would be slow to make decisions (being an expert at putting things off), and would rarely coach or advise them preferring to 'let them get on with their job'. Good teachers came and went under Mr Pogson's leadership and the team that remained became frustrated and disillusioned. I recognised Mr Pogson to be as much of a problem as Mr Bartlett.'

Now Tessa was once again annoyed by what she heard. Annoyed for the children. 'You had to do something, Mr James, you couldn't let that continue.'

Mr James smiled at Tessa's zeal; he was confidant that she would make a fine head teacher some day.

'But there was some good news Tessa. Let me tell you about Miss Belling. Miss Belling was an example of something quite different. Miss Belling is a plain speaker. You always know where you stand with her, she will tell you if she is happy and she will tell you if she is unhappy. You might not always like what you hear from Miss Belling, but if she is being critical she will criticise what you have done, not criticise you. When Miss Belling disciplines a pupil she will tell them just what it is she is disappointed with and why she herself feels let down. What she will never do is tell that pupil that he or she is not capable or indeed make any comment about that pupil's personality. On the other hand if Miss Belling is happy she will be the first to say so. I had seldom heard a teacher give so much praise before I met Miss Belling. She will constantly be pointing out to pupils exactly what they are doing well and telling them how pleased she is with them. I have sat in her classes and watched this, watched the same kids who are running riot for Mr Pogson, and are squeezing out barely adequate performances for Mr Bartlett, glowing with pride and straining at the leash to do well for Miss Belling. I have seen pupils clearly listening carefully to Miss Belling's praise for others and very obviously wanting such praise for themselves. So what do they do? They change their behaviour to get that praise. I can see that she gives far more praise than criticism, but when the criticism comes it's as if the praise has bought her the right to give criticism as well. But it doesn't stop with praise or criticism: she will always speak up when she has something to say. Miss Belling has disagreed with me on many occasions and yet I have never felt threatened or any lack of respect from her. In fact quite the opposite; I feel supported by her, she will put an alternative point of view clearly and will always accept my decision, whether I agree with her or not.'

'So watching Miss Belling was what really made you think about all this.'

'Yes Tessa, you are exactly right. It made me wonder what would happen in the school if I could get everyone behaving like this. Wouldn't people perform better if criticism was given and received easily? Wouldn't that help people to improve?

What if people always gave praise for a job well done? Wouldn't that make people happier and more confident?

What if people were prepared to express their views openly and respectfully, even when it meant disagreeing with someone else?'

Tessa could see exactly what Mr James meant 'Wouldn't that mean that bad ideas were stopped early and that good decisions were made more often?' she asked.

'That was just what I thought' said Mr James. 'What I saw in these three people was the past and the possible future of the school. I could see that the way people communicated with each other laid the foundation of the way our whole organisation worked. And I could see one other important thing: how the most powerful influencers were the people managers. I recognised that the change had to begin with me and then include all the other managers of people. I could see that things could only really change if I could get the behaviour of those people to be more like Miss Belling's and less like Mr Bartlett's and Mr Pogson's. If I could get that change to happen it would lead to a revolution! But I didn't envisage how powerful that revolution could be.'

Tessa was watching Mr James closely as he related his story. She could see a real passion in his eyes: he cared, really cared, and he was brimming with an infectious excitement. Perhaps this was the flush of success, the delight of achievement, the joy of making a positive difference. Whatever it was she knew that listening to him she was inspired to be a part of this success story. Much of what he was saying made complete sense to her; it was as if his account explained things she already knew but had not understood.

It also explained the coaching sessions she had with Miss Belling during her first few weeks at the school. As a new teacher, Tessa did not find this unusual, but with Mr James's explanation in mind she could see it as part of a strategy to get the whole school communicating in a particular way. Miss Belling was Head of Sport and Tessa was fortunate to be a member of her department. Miss Belling's guidance was about being *assertive*. She had talked to Tessa about *expressing her thoughts openly, using 'I' statements wherever possible,* avoiding any appearance of attacking someone else by criticising them. 'Always be firm Tessa but *criticise the behaviour not the person.*' Miss Belling had repeated this on several occasions pointing out how people defended themselves against verbal attack by becoming aggressive themselves or going quiet and holding a grudge that would affect their relationship in the future. As Mr James was describing Mr Bartlett's behaviour Tessa recalled this advice from Miss Belling. Miss Belling had also cautioned her about not speaking up, not expressing a view when she disagreed with something, not correcting behaviour she was unhappy with or not giving praise when it was due. Miss Belling called this passive and explained that this would cause just as many problems as being aggressive. Once again Tessa could now see that Mr James's description of Mr Pogson was of a person behaving passively. Miss Belling had shown Tessa how to be assertive and over the weeks that followed she would frequently advise Tessa on handling difficult situations with the words she might choose or how to hold her posture and facial expression to show an assertive stance. 'There's no point in saying to a pupil 'I'm unhappy with the standard of your work' when you look like you're scared or that you don't really care'. Miss Belling showed Tessa how *important* it was to *show* her *communication style as well as to speak it.*

Mr James interrupted Tessa's thoughts. 'Has that helped Tessa?'

'Yes,' she replied, 'I can see what was wrong, but how did you make the change happen?'

'At first I got some help. I found someone that specialised in teaching assertiveness and brought them into the school to work with myself and the other heads of department. It was an absolute revelation and I remember the faces of Mr Bartlett and Mr Pogson at our first meeting as our coach described three different behaviours that humans can adopt toward each other – *Aggressive, Passive or Assertive.* We all began to recognise how we use all three of these behaviours and how this influences the behaviour of others towards us, for better or for worse. With help, Mr Bartlett and Mr Pogson were able to understand what they were doing, how they were creating the behaviours around them, and how to change themselves. That was hard for them. Our coach became a mentor to them, helping them overcome some wrong ideas that they had carried in their heads for many years; and it worked. We learned to be optimistic about the capacity of people to change and that even people who look like they are firmly entrenched in wrong behaviours can change, given the right stimulation. How do Mr Bartlett and Mr Pogson seem to you?'

'I like them,' she replied. 'I didn't when I first arrived and thought that my opinion of them had changed simply because I had got to know them better.'

'Your time here began just after we confronted this and began to help people change. I think that your view of them has changed because they have changed.'

'Yes, I see that now. I remember Mr Bartlett scared me at the beginning. He once came bursting into one of my music lessons, he was very threatening. I was shocked at how the children changed the moment he came into the classroom. A few seconds earlier they had been open, smiling, laughing, learning. As soon as he appeared it was as if an invisible cord had been tightly drawn around their personalities, like a purse closed tight to protect the contents from a thief.'

'And now, Tessa? How do you find Mr Bartlett now?'

'Well,' Tessa hesitated, 'he is still a bit scarey at times...'

'You mean when you turn pupils purple?'

'Oh yes,' Tessa blushed. She had managed to push those thoughts to the back of her mind over the last few minutes 'but he is friendly now and has given me some useful advice.'

'And Mr Pogson?'

'It took us a little while to get over the Cream Pants episode.'

A mischievous grin sprang across Derek James's face.

'But now I really like him and the children seem to work much better with him. He doesn't fit the picture you described of him. Mr Pogson seems good at maintaining discipline; I overheard him in the playground yesterday telling a boy in no uncertain terms how disappointed he was with his test results. The boy looked him straight in the eye and apologised. I felt he would go away and try very hard not to let Mr Pogson down again'.

'Tessa, it's been a pleasant discussion but the bell will be going at any moment.'

'That's a shame,' said Tessa, 'you have just whetted my appetite. Surely that isn't all it took to change the school? What else are people doing differently? How did everyone react when you first spoke about this? What else did you do?'

'So many questions! The people influencers amongst us, led by me and the heads of department, are a key to the whole thing. I had to take responsibility for changing that group for the better. I made sure that we really understood what was wrong with our communication and how to put it right. I made sure that we all understood it so well that we could teach those for whom we were responsible and that they in turn could do the same with others. In other words this new understanding and these new skills in communication had to cascade through the whole organisation, starting from me. It had to pass through each line of responsible people all the way through to the pupils. What you see now is that process partially complete. We still have work to do.'

DRIIIIIIIIIIIING. The school bell rang to signify the end of lunch break.

'Time's up, Tessa. *Communication* was only *the first of the things that had to be changed*; there are a further four things that have been of critical importance. Maybe we will have a chance to discuss those on another occasion.'

Tessa and the Head Teacher had both got to their feet as the bell rang. As Derek opened his door they heard the school secretary talking on the telephone in the next office. 'Yes Mrs Basket, deep purple. No, Mrs Basket, I'm afraid the Head of Chemistry says it may take at least a week before it will wash off completely.'

'Have a great afternoon' said Mr James beaming widely as he turned back into his office. Tessa walked briskly through the outer office smiling sheepishly at the school secretary who mischievously winked at Tessa. As she left, her thoughts turned to Barry and Pogsy, and she wondered whether she would be able to teach them some of what she had learned. Perhaps a First Class Tigger day could, after all, be turned to their advantage.

Learning Questions

1. How and why did the world look different to Barry?
2. Which child and which teacher demonstrated passive behaviour?
3. What effect did Mr Bartlett have on the better teachers?
4. How did other pupils react to praise given by Miss Belling to one of their class mates?

Learning Summary - Assertive Communication

- We have three choices of communication style – Assertive, Passive and Aggressive
- Communication style is created by a mix of verbal and non verbal communication
- We can learn to be assertive by demonstrating certain non verbal communication and using certain words and word forms
- Aggressive behaviour causes a defensive response and undermines the confidence of those on the receiving end
- Passive behaviour frustrates the communicator and the person being communicated to

- The communication style of a team is dramatically affected by the communication style of the team leader
- Our communication style affects the way other people communicate with us – when it comes to communication we reap what we sow!

4

Snappy's Revenge
(Unlikely Leaders)

Part 1

'Hey look Steve, what's that?'

A purple bubble wobbled in the air and popped on the car windscreen as they drove through it. It left a perfectly circular eye that appeared to be staring at the two young men.

'Pollution in these industrial towns is a disgrace.'

'Yes Snappy, just keep your eye on the map and let's find this place,' replied Steve as he removed the offending bubble from screen and memory with his wiper blades.

'Ok, I've got it under control. Carry on along here, school to the right – full of screaming brats...park to the left – dodgy statue looks like a bloke holding a machine, turn next left, that's it...pass a row of shops – don't think I'll rush here for my Christmas shopping, library...next right up the hill, top of the road and it should be to the left.'

Steve steered his loaded estate car along the tidy residential streets into which Snappy had guided him. There was an industrious order about them, laid out in tidy rows and studded with churches, pubs and corner shops. These images conflicted with the television pictures he remembered from the time the rioting made headline news a few years ago. Sure enough, next left was West View Road. Neat houses lined either side, most fronted by small trim gardens. Not an expensive area, but it looked well maintained.

'Oh great, it's raining. We drive a hundred miles in sunshine and now it decides to rain.'

'Number 27 Snappy, look for number 27.'

'Uh oh, nutter alert. Look over there Steve. Some guy stood on the pavement in the rain, no shirt on, staring up into space. Why do they let them wander around like that?'

'Yes, Snappy, very sad but let me remind you we're making a series on leaders not nutters.'

Snappy was an experienced camera man. He had always loved taking pictures, hence his nickname; he was hooked on capturing life in pictures. At 26 he had already built himself a solid reputation but filming this series was the first time he'd worked with Steve. He'd enjoyed much of it, but Steve had some habits that annoyed him: he was often patronising, a bit full of himself and had a seriously bad habit of putting Snappy down in front of others. Nevertheless he had learned to ignore Steve's shortcomings and get on with the job; they had done pretty well together so far.

'Passing 39 on the left,' he replied, 'must be just a few down. There's 31, slow down Steve, that's 27 with the blue door.'

Steve squeezed the estate car into the one remaining parking space, switched off the engine and stretched. He would be pleased to get out of the car and get on with the job. This was Steve's first TV commission, a step up from the newspaper journalism that had been his livelihood to date. He really looked forward to these assignments, but needed this series to be good; it would either launch a lucrative new career or crush it before it had begun.

'You stay with the gear Snaps, I'll check out our contact.'

Steve opened the low wooden gate of number 27, walked the short distance to the front door and rang the modest push button bell. A slow grey rain fell as he glanced around him: a patch of lawn, some roses and a few shrubs – nothing remarkable. No reply, he rang again. Snappy had got out of the car and was opening up the back.

'Come on, come on,' Steve muttered to himself. 'Surely they haven't given us the wrong date.'

Research on a budget was asking for trouble – the team back at the office had got a brief wrong before. Still no reply, Steve walked to the side of the house looking for another door, but there was none.

'What's up?' called Snappy

'No one in Snaps, bloody research again. Better get them on the phone.' He turned back along the path. As Steve's hand touched the gate he heard a rattle at the house door and turned to see it slowly swung open by an elderly lady supporting herself on a stick.

'Hello dear,' she smiled, 'sorry I took so long, these legs don't work too well these days I'm afraid.'

Steve's jaw dropped

'You must be Steve?' continued the lady.

'Er, yes', stumbled Steve colouring a little and hoping she hadn't heard him cursing. 'I'm looking for Helen Lunn.'

'That's me dear, were you expecting someone older?' Was that a mischievous smile or just a mannerism wondered Steve.

'No, not at all,' he replied and regaining his poise returned to the door reaching out a hand to shake hers, then awkwardly withdrawing it realising that she couldn't respond and hold on to her stick and the door at the same time.

'I imagine you have some things to bring in so just make yourself at home.' She leaned on her stick to turn slowly back into the house 'I'll go and put the kettle on.'

Back at the car Snappy had unloaded the two flight cases that contained his camera and sound gear. 'OK boss?'

'Doesn't feel good Snappy.'

'Well if you will make a series called Unlikely Leaders.' Snappy's words were accompanied by a wry smile as he slammed the tailgate shut.

'Yes but not this unlikely! We've done ok so far but I reckon this is the dud. Anyhow we'll have to go through the motions now.'

'Well Snappy's instinct says this a goer.' He lifted the two cases, one in either hand.

'Good for Snappy,' said Steve locking the car with the electronic key fob.

'Take a bet on it?' asked Snappy turning to walk toward the house.

'A beer.'

'Boring,' starting to walk away from Steve.

'Two beers.'

'Double boring – where's your sense of adventure, Steve?'

Steve had started to follow but paused to consider the options, and then grinned.

'OK Snaps, when we find out this story is a dud you cut off that ridiculous pony tail.'

Now it was Snappy who stopped in his tracks. He frowned as he considered an appropriate response. Then he too grinned.

'OK, but if it's a goer you lose that rat on your lip you call a moustache. Done?'

'But what about my public, they won't recognise me!' Steve posed for an imaginary press corps.

'Well I haven't exactly seen the hoards following us down the street for your autograph. So are we having the bet?' Snappy turned and held Steve with an enquiring gaze.

'Alright I suppose so, at least it will liven up a wet day in the middle of nowhere.'

In her cozy sitting room Helen had eased herself back into a comfortable armchair. All was neat. The room looked and smelled clean. The furniture was old but well cared for, there were photographs of presumably her late husband, her children and grandchildren; nothing to suggest anything other than a simple life. Snappy was unpacking the cases and Steve sat opposite Helen opening his briefcase and taking in the surroundings with an experienced eye.

'Helen, thank you very much for giving us your time like this. I have prepared a list of questions that I thought you could take a look through before we get started on the interview.'

'That would be delightful dear, I would love to look through each and every question... but I can't.'

Both Steve and Snappy looked at her inquiringly.

'Why not, Helen?'

'Because I'm registered blind dear. I can see only blurs and I'm afraid these days I can't read a thing.'

Steve looked at Snappy and winked, making a pretend pair of scissors with his fingers and snipping at a pretend ponytail on the back of his own head. Snappy got busy with his camera.

'Alright Helen, we'll just get ourselves ready and then go for a question and answer session and see how we get on.'

Helen's tragic loss of eyesight brought with it a sharpened clarity in her mind's eye. As she sat waiting for her visitors to ready themselves her memories graphically engulfed her thoughts.

She had lived her entire life in this town brought up just two streets away from West View Road. Her father had worked at The Factory and her childhood memories were of a warm family environment. These memories were decorated with other families and children and those who were still alive remained friends. She recalled how every child in the neighbourhood looked forward to the Christmas parties at The Factory when the factory managers would fill a great hall full of flags, balloons, and music. Or in the summer, the street's residents would get together and hire a coach to go to the seaside or out into the hills and meadows of the country. Those were great days of happiness and friendship. And in the light of her later experiences what she particularly remembered were the people who seemed to make things happen.

From her school years she could clearly recall the Head Teacher. The school was popular and well respected and she did well there. She was the first member of her family to go to university and gain a degree. As the school declined in later years she saw the difference made by new Head Teachers or as she now recognised that role, the School Leader.

She remembered the Silver Band, the youth band that she joined and in particular she remembered Mrs Jones, the lady that seemed to make it all happen. They travelled around the country to compete with other bands and even competed abroad – unforgettable experiences. Most of the kids spent hour upon hour practising and rehearsing, their success made national headlines and those involved felt special. But after Mrs Jones retired it was never the same again.

Helen remembered her father's manager at The Factory and how everyone worked so hard for him. Everyone in The Town knew of Alan Mars, The Factory's owner, of what he had done and how well he was respected.

Mr James was a neighbour who, her parents told her, had led the project to build The Town's library and reading rooms. Mr James had gathered a team of people who worked tirelessly to raise funds. Alan Mars had matched the money raised in The Town and the opening day of the library was a day that Helen remembered with pride. She could recall holding her mother's hand and waving a flag outside the grand new stone building that was to bring reading to the ordinary person, at a time when books were prohibitively expensive. Helen remembered the cheering, the speeches and Mr James patting her on the head and saying 'it's youngsters like you that will benefit from this,' and benefit she did.

When Helen's working life began she found her first employers in another town. She remembered her shock at the disrespect and lack of interest in the company's work shown by so many employees. But she could now also see that the leader of the business did little to earn respect from those employees. Both were losers.

What Helen saw was that leaders surround us and that they constantly influence us. She saw also that when we become leaders it is as if we are given an undirected and powerful weapon. We influence for good or bad, whether we intend to or not.

She saw that we all watch leaders and as leaders we are watched. In times of challenge, eyes and minds turn to the leader, but even in docile days the leader remains a surreptitious focus of attention.

The manager, the boss, and the organiser – we watch them for whatever it is we need from them, but even when we appear to need nothing we still watch. Such must be the burden of the leader to be so constantly under inspection that actions of insignificance can have an impact far beyond their intent.

Over her working life Helen found herself managed by managers both bad and good and when she became a manager herself she was fortunate to work for a boss who took the time to explain to her just how leadership worked. So it was that when Helen's turn came to lead others, she did well. She was popular, she got great results through those that worked for her and she progressed within the organisation.

As Helen's career developed, she was saddened by what happened at The Factory and, it seemed to her as a direct result, what happened to the town that she loved. It was like a ripple effect emanating from The Town's greatest employer. Her father passed away shortly before The Factory began its decline, and as redundancies hit, unemployment in The Town grew. The Town's character began to change. Some people moved to find work elsewhere but most stayed and those people seemed to change. What was once smart and shiny became neglected and unkempt, people without work seemed to lose purpose. Streets that had been proud and well kept started to show gardens that were overgrown and houses in need of repair. Shops began to close on the high street, kids vandalised statues and gardens. Voluntary organisations began to lose members and disappear. The Silver Band lasted a few short years after Mrs Jones's retirement but then closed – people lost interest. As Helen progressed through her working life and learned more about leadership she saw that The Town was crying out for leadership that it did not get.

West View was the area where Helen had always lived. It held the streets were she had grown up with her friends. But as Helen reached her fifties and her own career blossomed, she saw West View decline so badly that even she had thought of moving away. Gangs of purposeless kids terrorised some areas, corner shops were barred or closed and boarded, cars weren't safe on the streets, and many of the older people felt like prisoners in their homes, not daring to stray beyond their front doors.

This decline culminated in the riots that hit the news headlines. One hot summer evening a devil's brew of young people with too little to occupy themselves and lives that seemed to offer little purpose, mixed with a crowd of troublemakers from another town, too much alcohol and a hot night – brought fire, destruction and anger to the streets of this once successful and popular town. The decline was complete and the humiliation for those for whom The Town had once been a place of pride was deep and devastating.

It was at this time that Helen's life was hijacked by her health, an unexpected turn of events for an active person, a change that took her by surprise. She was equally unprepared to discover that becoming a pensioner would be the start of a new adventure.

She didn't want to stop working but the erosion of her eyesight was rapid and cruel. 'Macular degeneration' diagnosed the specialist, 'unusual in a lady of your age.' This swift decline rendered reading without a magnifying glass impossible within 6 months of her retirement, and reading with one equally impossible within another 6 months. The stroke took away the strength in her legs but fortunately left the rest of her in reasonable shape. Within 12 months of her 58th birthday she had become a pensioner with significant disability. Given this background it was particularly remarkable that in the 10 years since her retirement Helen had led the successful regeneration of West View.

'OK Helen, are you ready?' Steve had sorted his notes and questions, and Snappy was prepared, camera focussed and ready to role.

'Do you mind if I just pop to the loo before we start dear?' said Helen, already easing herself up with her sticks.

'Of course not,' said Steve in his most charming tone of voice whilst, now aware of Helen's blindness, winking at Snappy and stroking his moustache with pride.

Part 2

The game! The Game! THE GAME! – Lively music bounces around the bright pictures that deliver the advertising message.

It is nine months later; Steve is at home sitting in front of a television with his girlfriend, Sarah.

'Why do you want to watch this Steve? You're normally fed up with these programmes by the time they reach the screen.'

'I know but this one is different. I'm really pleased with this one.'

The advertisement finishes and is replaced with the announcer's voice – 'In this final episode of the series 'Unlikely Leaders', investigative journalist Steve Prince meets perhaps the unlikeliest leader of the series and...loses his moustache.'

' And not before time,' Sarah giggles.

'Hush.'

The title music and standard intro sequence runs, followed with archive news footage of rioting.

Steve's voice is heard: 'Five years ago these scenes hit our television screens, as this once respectable and prosperous town descended into chaos.'

Riot footage gives way to a shot of Steve (with moustache) standing in a respectable leafy street.

'Today I am here to discover how a neighbourhood that had plumbed such depths could, in a matter of a few years, have turned into this.'

Camera pans down respectable street and toward an attractive leafy park.

'But it is not really the 'how' that I am interested in but the 'who'. Who made this change happen and what did they do to make it happen? Was there a single driving force, a leader, and if there was, what is the secret of their success? We have already met, in this series of short films, a number of unusual individuals who have demonstrated leadership. But today I have come to meet the most surprising of those leaders. Today I have come to meet sixty-eight year old Helen Lunn, virtually blind and crippled by a stroke, and to explore how she led this neighbourhood from this...' more newsreel of rioting, neatly showing a Molotov cocktail arching through the air and landing with a burst of flame at the feet of a line of policemen...to this.' The image returns to Steve standing in the respectable street.

'When I first met Helen Lunn my reaction was that she could not possibly be the leader responsible for this transformation. I was wrong. In making this film I have learned how a blind and partially crippled pensioner galvanised a whole neighbourhood into positive action and that this is a remarkable lesson in the working of leadership. The first stage in my enquiry was to talk to some of those who have taken part in this extraordinary adventure.'

The picture changes to a bar, a meeting has apparently just finished. The camera view is moving to a group sat at a table, Steve's voice is heard 'Excuse me, can I interrupt you for a few minutes?' Various members of the group smile and make space for Steve to join them.

'You have just finished working on the new playground project. I am interested to know what role Helen played in this?'

A young fair haired man asks 'What do you mean? Helen could hardly get stuck in to the building work could she?' Laughter follows amongst the group.

'No, that's my point,' replies Steve, 'I understand that between you, you prepared and submitted the grant application, you liased with the local authority, you even organised the ground clearing and construction work.'

'Yes that's right'

'So Helen wasn't involved at all?'

A few of the group nod in agreement. But another replies: 'Well hold on.' It's the fair headed man again. 'Helen chaired the meeting when the idea came up, I know because it was my idea. Helen asked me to explain more, encouraged me to follow it through, suggested the names of some others that I could invite to join a team.'

'That's right,' a balding middle aged man speaks, 'she rang me and asked if I would like to help with the grant application.'

'Had you made a grant application before?' asks Steve

'No, I was out of work but had been a journalist for a while. She thought I might be able to learn to do the application.'

'And did you?'

'Oh yes, it took a while but once I got to know how, it wasn't too difficult.'

'And she suggested one or two others that are sat around this table,' the fair headed man was speaking again. 'She got us to draw up a written plan of exactly what we wanted to do, I read it to her and she asked me loads of questions which made me think of all sorts of details that I had missed.'

'OK,' Steve again, 'so how involved would you say she was?'

'Well she helped me set up the team; she encouraged me when I needed it; she got us to run proper meetings and encouraged us to develop our ideas and then write them down clearly so that we could explain them effectively to other people.'

The scene cuts to a second such interview and then a third – a middle aged couple discussing the success of a neighbourhood-watch scheme, some teenagers talking about how they had started to run skate boarding sessions for local kids and then went on to design and build a skate area in the local park – a consistent theme began to emerge.

Helen was never directly involved in doing the tasks that had changed this neighbourhood, but in all cases she clearly helped pick the right people to be involved, encouraged people to develop themselves and be ambitious, made sure tasks were defined clearly and understood, and got people to work together as teams. It seemed from these interviews that many pairs of hands and active minds had achieved the regeneration of this neighbourhood. What also seemed remarkable was that these were the same people who had been living in the neighbourhood in the bad times. Somehow they had changed, and it looked as if Helen was the unlikely source of that change.

Steve appears on screen facing the camera.

'Try as I might, I have found no other leader lurking behind the scenes. It's time to talk to Helen and ask her directly if she thinks she is responsible for all that has happened here and, if so, just how she has done it.'

The scene cuts to Helen's lounge where she is sitting in her comfortable chair.

Steve's voice: 'Helen, I've been checking up on you.'

'Sounds serious,' she replies smiling. You can see clearly on camera that her eyes don't function, there is no life in them, but the rest of her face is full of expression and personality.

'There is no doubt that you are regarded as the leader of this community, and yet I don't see how you do it. If I may be blunt, you are a lady who cannot see, can hardly walk and yet manages to extend an extraordinary influence. Can you tell me how?'

'Yes,' comes the bluff reply. 'Leadership is something that can be learned and I hope that what I tell you will be helpful to others.'

Helen adjusts her position awkwardly, this looks to be an uncomfortable manoeuvre, but she is preparing herself to talk.

'As a young woman leaders always intrigued me. I watched them with interest and as I got older I found myself placed in a position where I was responsible for leading others. I was made a manager. I quickly understood why so many get it wrong because at first I got it horribly wrong. I did what I thought would make people happy and therefore make them work for me, but I simply became frustrated and found myself working longer and longer hours to get the job done. At the same time my relationship with my team members got worse not better. But I was lucky, my own manager stepped in and told me what he had learned about management and leadership. What he said helped me make sense of so much that I had seen in the successful and unsuccessful leaders I had observed in my life. I found that by putting into practise what he told me, I became a successful leader.

'What he told me is based upon the idea of needs. What do you understand by a need Steve?'

The camera shot pans out to include both Steve and Helen in the picture.

Steve replies: 'I suppose it's something that you want, a lot.'

'Give me an example,' says Helen

'Well...,' Steve furrows his brow in thought... 'I need a beer after a long hard days work.'

'A need is something you must have, rather than something you want.'

'Yup, definitely a beer,' replies Steve with a smile on his face.

'You want a beer Steve, but you could get by without one. You need a drink and water would suffice. And that's the critical difference between a want and a need. A want is something that we would like whilst a need is something we cannot do without – we need oxygen to live, without it we die. We need a roof above our heads although we want a nice house that suits our tastes.'

'I get it,' says Steve. 'My teenage sister keeps telling our dad that she needs a car to get to school, in fact she wants a car and needs a bus pass. But what has this to do with Leadership?'

'It's critical Steve just stay with me for a moment. How would you explain what leadership is?'

'Just a minute Helen, I'm supposed to be asking the questions.'

'Yes dear, but by asking you questions I can help you understand better. How would you explain what leadership is?'

'I suppose it's when a person is followed by others.'

'Good, that's a nice simple answer. Think of the old children's game of follow my leader; a leader is a leader as long as the others are following, you remember in that game the leader does all sorts of strange things and the followers are supposed to copy. Actually that's not too far from real life, since a leader is often the only person who has the big picture and frequently asks people to do unfamiliar things – in other words, to change. The test of leadership is whether people follow.'

'Right Helen, so how does this fit with needs?'

'Because groups of people have needs that must be satisfied if they are to work together – we can call them Group Needs. Now here's a simple statement of fact: people will follow whoever satisfies those Group Needs.'

Helen sits back in her chair and silence follows, she is clearly waiting for a response from Steve.

Steve seems disappointed 'Is that it?'

'In simple terms, yes,' replies Helen. 'A leader is someone who satisfies Group Needs. The group don't make a conscious choice, if someone is satisfying these needs they will follow that person, although there is one other element that is important: they must also exhibit certain personality traits.'

The camera shows Steve's face. He is clearly listening intently.

'Steve, leadership concerns respect, respect for the leader by the followers. A successful leader has built a high level of respect amongst the followers – respect is built or undermined by how well the leader satisfies Group Needs. Where respect is high, then followers will follow, where respect is low, they will not.'

The camera view has panned out to show both Steve and Helen.

'What this means is that where you have someone who has a leadership title but a low level of respect, that person will not truly be the leader. The evidence might be when this person tries to introduce some change into the team but the team does not follow, they do not embrace the change. Going back to my example of the children's game, this would be like the leader continuing in front carrying out actions to be followed, but all the others have stood back and are just watching this leader trotting around looking foolish. The leader is no longer leading. When this happens in the workplace an unofficial leader often emerges, perhaps a stronger member of the team. In fact, look carefully and you will see that such a person is simply satisfying Group Needs more effectively than the person with the title of manager.'

'So Helen, you have *a formula for building respect and*

becoming an effective leader which is to *satisfy Group Needs and exhibit certain personality traits.'*

'Yes, that's it.'

'Are you going to tell me what those Groups Needs are?'

'Of course, that's the lesson that leaders must learn – they must know what to do. The way I was taught this was to divide these needs into three areas, it makes them easier to remember.'

The camera has begun to slowly move toward Helen. As she continues to speak her animated face gradually fills the entire screen.

'The first of those three to consider are *Individual Needs*. This group of needs is about awakening each individual within the group and preparing them to give their very best. Each person needs to feel that they are recognised and treated as an individual different from everybody else. A successful leader therefore gets to know each person in the group, *recognises individual abilities and uses individual skills.* You have spoken with people from West View who were unemployed but each had a skill to be found and built on. Someone was needed to take an interest in each person and help that skill come out. Some of our youngsters have gone back to college to learn things so that they can contribute to what we have been doing in West View. So amongst these Individual Needs is also a need to be *trained and developed.* If people are to give of their best they need always to be learning, growing and developing. The Leader needs to make sure that this happens. They also need to receive *praise* and be given *status.* These are easy things to do as long as the leader plans and remembers to do them. Find reasons to praise people by observing them doing things well, and status can be given simply by asking people's opinions and advice. A leader needs to be sure to *involve every person.* As soon as someone is left out of the group's plans and activity, that person will begin to slide away from working in the team. Just one other Individual Need that a leader must satisfy is to show a human face and *acknowledge personal problems*. This doesn't mean try to solve them, but simply by acknowledging their existence leadership is shown; by ignoring them as if they do not exist then we are treating the person as just another body in the workplace rather than as an individual. These things are Individual Needs.'

Now the camera view pans out showing the two of them sitting face to face.

'Remember that word 'needs' Steve, these are all needs. People need these things from a leader in order to work together as a team. Whoever fulfils these needs will be regarded as the leader.'

'But Helen, I can see that something like praise is desirable, but people exist without it. I think most people get far less praise than they would like – surely praise is a want not a need.'

'Good point, but praise is a need if people are to work together and follow a leader. Of course people exist without praise, but in order to work to their best capacity I can assure you that real meaningful praise, not just a 'well done', is not optional it is a need.'

'Yes, I take your point,' said Steve. 'If I think about my own response to genuine praise, it is powerful.'

'The Second area of Group Needs is *Team Needs*. These are about getting individuals to work together as a team and about individuals taking on a group identity as team members.'

Scenes around West View have been edited into the film, and as Helen speaks we see a children's playground, a community hall buzzing with activity, a busy skateboard park and more. Helen's voice continues over these images.

'When any group works together they must share *common standards*. The leader must make sure that those common standards exist and that they are observed by every member of the group – in other words the leader must maintain *discipline* around these common standards. An example of a leader neglecting this is when a blind eye is turned to a group member who persistently arrives late. The level of respect for the leader amongst the other team members will decline. In this circumstance you could define a clear fault in leadership.

A leader must also make sure that *communication amongst the team* is assertive as often as possible. The leader cannot ignore poor communication; the leader must step in and do something about it. The leader must bring the team together by *encouraging and motivating* them to work as a team and the leader must make sure that a *team spirit* builds between the team members. Finally the leader must *obtain agreement* from those team members to the *tasks and targets* that the team undertakes.'

The picture changes to show both Helen and Steve sitting opposite each other.

'In reality, these were not difficult things to achieve at West View. Through good work on Individual Needs many people were in the right state of mind to begin working in teams. The very first team we created sat down at a meeting that I chaired and began by agreeing common standards for how we would work together. Meeting times, making notes, reporting to others, public statements, holding money; it was a long list because I had asked all of the team members to think about this before they came to the meeting. They came with ideas of things that they thought were important, and we discussed them. The very act of doing this began to build a team spirit and by the time we had finished that first meeting we had devised our own set of team standards that everyone understood and agreed with. All I had done was to bring people together and chair the meeting so that it ran well. Everyone got their say, but the rest of the team members did everything else.'

'Occasionally I find a need to talk to someone about a slip in standards and I always do that promptly and clearly. Sometimes I have had to speak to team members about the way they have been communicating. At one meeting one of the team became aggressive. I adjourned the meeting for a few minutes and spoke to the person concerned outside and in private. I said, 'I need your help. I am unhappy with you raising your voice and calling other team members names, the effect is to make others reluctant to speak and to raise emotions that get in the way of reaching good decisions. This means that the meeting is less likely to reach a useful conclusion and I will have failed as the chair. I understand that you may be upset but I would like you to speak assertively if you disagree and to respect other people's right to disagree with you assertively.' This type of approach is usually effective at making someone reflect on inappropriate behaviour. In this instance the other person apologised and spent the rest of the meeting working hard to help the meeting achieve a good solution, for which I thanked them afterwards. As a leader it was important that I dealt with this and was seen to deal with this by the other team members.'

'This is fascinating Helen, I am beginning to see how a leader satisfies Group Needs. Previously in this series we have observed successful leaders but your analysis of exactly how you have succeeded is invaluable. You said there were three sets of Group Needs, what is the third?'

'Glad you're paying attention Steve,' Helen said, her smile overcoming her empty eyes. 'The third area of Group Needs are all about the job in hand, about whatever the team has been formed to do. I call these *Task Needs*. Have you ever had the experience of working for a boss who never made it absolutely clear what you were expected to do? Or who didn't share the work out fairly amongst the team, perhaps consistently giving the more interesting tasks to favourites? Or a boss that seemed to take little interest in the quality of what you were doing?'

Steve smiled. 'You must have been following my career. But yes, I have come across all of those things, in fact you are making me think about people that I have worked for in the past, I can see why the good ones were good and the bad ones were bad.'

'And what about respect Steve? What level of respect did you have for the manager who neglected the things we have been talking about?'

'Oh very low, I have no doubt about that answer.'

'And that's because that person was failing to fulfil your Group Needs.'

'Yes I can see that.'

The camera makes a single shot on Helen, slowly zooming in on her face once again as she speaks.

'So, Steve, Task Needs are the things we all need from a team leader with regard to the work that the team is to do. A leader must *define the task* clearly so all understand just what is to be achieved and then the leader must make sure that there is *a plan* to achieve that task so that all team members know how the task is to be carried out. The leader must *allocate the work* fairly and sensibly amongst the team members and then set standards and *monitor the quantity and quality* of that work, taking action if those standards are not maintained. We also rely upon our leader to *check performance against the plan* and where necessary *adjust the plan* to avoid failure.'

The camera returns to show Steve.

'So the secret of leadership is to satisfy the Group Needs of those you want to lead?'

Once again the camera view alters to show them both.

'That is just about right but there is one other thing that you must achieve if you want people to follow you. We have so far discussed what you must do, we must also consider how you do it.

By that I mean the character traits that you display to those that you are leading. In a way, the two go hand in hand because it is difficult to satisfy Group Needs without displaying these traits, but if you watch successful leaders with this list in mind you will see all of them displayed.'

'I'm poised note book in hand Helen, give me the list.'

'You make me sound like a college lecturer, but after you have used these things for a while you do remember them. I'm afraid I'm a long way past writing anything down myself.'

'Well treat me as a beginner Helen and put me out of my suspense. What is this list of *character traits* that is so important to leaders?'

Shots of people and faces taken around the streets of West View have been edited into the film and are shown as Helen speaks.

'Let's start with *humility and warmth* since perhaps those are not the ones you are most anticipating. Humility is the opposite of arrogance and an overbearing ego, it is demonstrated by a willingness to listen and to admit fault. Warmth is about using the heart as well as the mind, taking genuine interest in people and showing pleasure and friendship.'

'Alongside these must sit *integrity and toughness*. Integrity is honesty, it is the quality that makes people trust you, it is doing what you say or quickly acknowledging when you find you are unable to do as you have promised. To be tough means not to shrink from difficult or unpleasant tasks, being prepared to be firm and assertive with people. There are times when we have to deliver bad news, make unpleasant decisions, insist on what you believe in.

61

'The tough leader must take care to bring *fairness* to decisions and actions. To be even-handed, treating each team member with equal opportunity. Fairness is to be just and unbiased.

'Since leaders must inspire at times, then *enthusiasm* is a necessity. If a leader is not enthusiastic about something then how can the leader expect the team members to be enthusiastic? But leaders must remember that enthusiasm is demonstrated by actions, by facial expression, tone of voice, the way people carry themselves. For someone like me who is restricted in physical movement I must rely more on tone of voice, carefully chosen words and use of my hands.

The camera view returns to a full shot of Helen's face as she talks.

'Finally it must be obvious that leaders should show *confidence*, and yet unlike the character traits that I have just described, which can all be consciously learned and developed, confidence is something that builds naturally and cannot be quickly created by a simple change of behaviour. You will find that what builds confidence is knowledge. You, Steve, will be confident in making a film because you know how to do it, your camera man confident in using his camera because he knows its workings well, but place you in an unfamiliar situation and your confidence will decline (whatever you might show on the surface). So confidence comes with knowledge, and the more a leader learns to satisfy needs and demonstrate appropriate character traits the more confident he or she will become.'

Helen stops talking. After a short pause, Steve speaks. The camera view once again shows them both.

'So that's it?'

'Yes.'

'That's the secret of how West View became regenerated?'

'Oh no Steve, what I have told you is what makes

leadership work. But that is only a part of what has happened at West View. Good Leadership is a vital piece in the puzzle, but not the only thing. Remember I told you about the importance of maintaining Assertive Communication throughout the team? That's another vital piece. There are others, but I think perhaps that is for another time, don't you?'

'Helen thank you for taking the time to explain so much to me, now I have a confession and an apology to make to you.'

Helen cocks her head, an inquiring expression on her face.

Steve continues: 'When I first arrived here, I was so convinced that you could not be the leader of this community revival, that I made a small wager to that effect with my cameraman. I have of course been proved wrong. Your story and what you have told us has been extraordinary and invaluable.'

'Oh dear, I hope I haven't cost you too much,' replies Helen 'Just my moustache.'

'You have a moustache? I'm sure you will look better without it.'

'Helen Lunn, thanks for allowing us into your home and your story, and for your lesson in leadership.'

Music and end titles begin.

'That was great' said Sarah. 'She really is an interesting character with a fascinating story.'

'Yes and I was curious to know what the other pieces in the puzzle were, but we ran out of time. Perhaps there's a subject for another series. I might put that idea forward.'

On the television screen two pictures of Steve appear, one with and one without a moustache. 'Ha ha, very good Snappy,' sneered Steve, 'I don't know why he's allowed to get involved with the editing.'

Suddenly Steve sits upright. 'Bloody Snappy,' he yells.

The pictures of Steve had been replaced by a closing shot

in Helen's sitting room; the camera zooms in on a framed photograph. The photograph had not been there when Steve conducted the interview. It shows Helen looking very smart, sitting in a wheelchair receiving a presentation from a well known member of the royal family.

'He hid that picture.' Steve is standing up and pointing at the screen.

'Hid what Steve?' asked Sarah

'That picture, he hid it in case it made me change my mind about the bet. He knew all along that she was the real leader'.

'I think he did you a favour Steve,' said Sarah 'it's something that will help people remember you. You'll be 'The guy on TV who bet his moustache rather than another faceless TV journalist whose name no one can remember.'

'Yes that's a point,' said Steve stroking his shaven lip and checking his profile in the mirror.

Music and titles fade. Steve points the remote control at the TV and zaps. The picture disappears and the screen goes black, except for a small purple bubble that remains at the centre for a few seconds and then disappears.

Learning Questions

1. Mr James and Mrs Jones are instances of what?
2. What is the point of using the example of a blind and crippled lady?
3. Why is Helen's distinction between a need and a want important?
4. What are Individual needs?
5. How did Helen's examples of good leaders create a 'ripple effect' beyond the team itself?

Learning Summary – Team Leadership

- We can learn to lead
- A team is a group of people helping each other toward a common goal
- A group needs specific things from a leader if they are to become a team
- It is helpful to remember these needs in three categories - task, team and individual needs
- The person who fulfils those needs will be regarded as the leader by the team
- By learning to fulfil certain needs and display certain characteristics we will encourage people to respect and follow us

5

The Game
(Helping Each Other to Learn)

Part 1

From her position on the coach's rostrum, elevated four metres above the pitch, Alice felt full exposure to the roar that was triggered as the ball found the net. Single yells and shrieks combined to form one almighty wave of sound, individuals vanished to be replaced by something formidable that bore no resemblance to the 40,000 separate parts of which it consisted. The Gamescreens, which linked in an unbroken circle capping the top tiers of each of the stands, burst into a multicoloured carnival of images as they registered the score. The 3D sound system, delivering perfect digital sound to every inch of the stadium, pumped blasts of energetic triumphant celebration. To be in the stadium at this moment was to be in the centre of a sensory detonation. This, like other aspects of The Game, had been shrewdly designed to create an addictive thrill that captured audiences of a size that live sport had not seen for many decades.

This great arena of light and sound, home to The Mechanics, formed a complete and impressive oval, a towering yet graceful addition to The Town's skyline.

Three sides of the stadium were packed with people who were now on their feet; on the fourth the visiting followers were subdued but, in the spirit of this world-dominating sport, applauded the skilful play that had led to the spectacular strike.

Both teams were running back to position for the next start – AutoRef did not allow for lingering and a wrongly positioned player at the restart would earn an automatic penalty drive for the other side.

Alice gazed around the stadium, this centrepiece of the West View regeneration, and thought how incredible it was that such a place existed. Just a decade ago towns like this would muster five or six thousand at best to see a football or a rugby match, but the advent of The Game had sent such memories rapidly retreating into the past. In a few short years, new technologies had created new possibilities whilst corruption and greed had become endemic in the old games and made them vulnerable. The rise of The Game had been overwhelming.

The AutoRef siren set the match in motion again. Alice focussed on her players. In her view they were an outstanding team: not the most skilful players she had seen, but their team working was exemplary. Six males and six females played on either gender-separated side of the pitch, their observation of each other had to be perfect with play limited to 20 seconds without transfer of the ball to the other side. A disorganised team would endlessly lose possession by falling into this 'wrong side' trap. This team's confidence in each other's ability and play of strategies was manifested in their actions on the pitch. For example, long passes sweeping the ball forty or fifty metres would be made without visual contact, stunning opponents and creating scoring opportunities from apparently sterile circumstances.

In Alice's eyes the key was coaching, by which she meant individuals helping each other to learn. Alice's title was Team Coach and she believed her role to be making coaching happen. It did not matter whether she coached, whether team members coached other team members, or indeed if team members coached Alice. What Alice had worked hard to achieve was a willingness to coach and be coached by all.

This in turn led to the continued development of all team members. The players recognised that skills did not stay sharp without constant attention; it also meant that they were regularly developing new skills. Players met outside the organised group coaching sessions that Alice arranged to help each other build new skills, and as a result Alice saw them moving forward in their abilities at a stunning pace. It was common for some of the team to develop new ideas for plays, moves or strategies and bring them to a team meeting. Consequently the team always seemed to be innovating, developing and trying new ideas. This brought a willingness to face and embrace change, and made for a team always looking for the new play, always seeking to challenge existing ways.

Alice had previously seen young players become quickly set in their ways. Youngsters in their early twenties protecting old habits with a 'this is the way we've always done it' approach. She had learned that when this happened, individuality and creativity was stifled while confidence became fragile. This was why you would observe a seesawing performance from players within the space of a single match; a success would breed immediate and obvious confidence, whilst a set back could quickly deflate those same players. She had seen teams destroy themselves by this simple yet subtle method.

Alice recognised that her growing experience had led her to these understandings. She knew that this team was performing in such an impressive way because she had created the circumstances where such a coaching habit could flourish.

These players also knew how to please a crowd, and as such they enjoyed some of the best incomes in the league thanks to the clever design of The Game by The Game League, who dictated payment rules. Each player was paid the same wage by the club irrespective of skill, performance or length of service. This was a set proportion of the gate and media income specified by The Game League and that proportion was precisely the same at every club. The more successful a club was at attracting an audience, the more the players got paid. It paid to play an attractive game.

But it was the bonus that made the difference coming directly from the crowds in the stands. The clubs derived a major part of their income through the 5,000 gaming points that formed an integral part of the stadium design. These automated machines displayed odds, received bets and paid out winnings. Critically, they also offered a second function allowing the crowd to pay players for their performance. The huge Gamescreens carried the ever changing gaming odds on every aspect of the game: first to score, time of score, final score, second to score, total attendance... a lengthy list of possibilities tempted a steady flow of finance from the crowd. In addition, the screens carried a running total of the amounts paid by the crowd for each player and the players could see this too. This design did everything possible to ensure that players played to the best of their ability and to please the crowd.

Alice tensed as her captain, Jules, executed a perfect tackle to gather the ball and, in what appeared to be a single flowing and athletic action, swung her stick hard and drove the ball in a curving arch horizontally across the pitch to The Spider who was in clear ground. As the ball travelled, a single game screen on each side of the ground tracked its progress to the millimetre. The image was generated by the AutoRef receiving a signal from the transmitter inside the ball plotting it onto a computer generated, but absolutely accurate reproduction of the pitch. There was a swell of expectation from around the ground, the position looked good and The Spider was a centre driver in form.

He gathered the ball in both hands and sprinted toward the opposing end, side stepping one opponent and then releasing the ball to The King before a crunching tackle brought him to the ground. The King executed a set piece to perfection on hearing a coded shout from Jules. The ball passed so fast between three players that the opponents had little chance of anticipating the play and the third player delivered it to the feet of Little Lulu in front of a yawning goal. As she raised her foot to drive the ball into the net her standing leg was swept from under her, sending her sprawling on her face. Immediately the AutoRef siren wailed. The stadium was bathed in red flashing light as the Gamescreens first signalled a penalty and then showed the incident from three angles to confirm the computerised decision. The 3D began to pulse a low note as AutoRef allowed the allotted time for the ball to be placed.

Jules always took the penalties. She stepped up and placed the ball before the countdown started. 5, 4, 3 – the crowd were chanting the numbers as they appeared on the screens, the pulsing note rose in volume as the count progressed 2, 1 ... Jules swept at the ball. She had chosen to drop into the Top Net, a high risk move since, although the Top Net was unprotected, the gap was only a meter square and the ball had to be lofted over a 6 metre high barrier made of some transparent but solid material. The ball rose high into the air, far higher than it needed to... she hadn't just chosen high risk; she had chosen to be audaciously theatrical. At about 9 meters the ball began to drop. For a moment the stadium was frozen in silence as every pair of eyes tracked a descent that began in slow motion, as gravity overcame Jules's drive and then accelerated, the ball flying toward its target.

The action was in front of the Helen Lunn stand, so for those at the other end of the stadium the Gamescreens were showing the standard three camera angles on alternate screens. The ball hit the Top Net space as if carefully placed at the precise centre with the aid of a tape measure. It shot through the gap into the net, the detonation of sound that followed almost overwhelming the siren that acknowledged the score and ended the match. Jules glanced at the Gamescreens to see her Match Bonus rushing upwards rewarding her high-risk approach to the penalty.

Alice wandered back out onto the pitch. She had congratulated her team on another first class performance, and completed her match notes for tomorrow's coaching session. All was quiet now, just a few last reluctant fans being ushered out of the ground by marshals. Despite the good result Alice was troubled. It wasn't one big thing; it was a bunch of niggling irritations that together worried her. She looked up at the Gamescreens and could see that three or four of them were not working. This didn't make a big difference to the overall effect since there were forty individual screens making up the full oval, but nevertheless it shouldn't be like that. She had heard groups of fans grumbling about the long queues for drinks, the poor state of the toilets, the difficulty in getting a programme. She had been disappointed by some disorganisation around hotel booking for their last away match, and this was not the first time that the club's administration had let her down. This handful of incidents had set her mind along this critical track and now, as she considered them, she could think of an alarming number of other examples. In particular she reflected that apart from match days there were few smiling faces around the club. The place seemed to have lost its spark, despite her team's performances. Alice knew that however well her team performed, if the club let them down it would ultimately effect their motivation and their play.

As she considered these issues she reached a decision. This team was without doubt the best she had ever worked with, and this season was a great opportunity to win a major trophy for the first time in her coaching career. She would not allow poor organisation at the club to ruin it; tomorrow she would confront the Managing Director.

A thump on the back brought her thoughts back to the here and now. 'Come on boss, haven't you seen enough of this pitch?' It was Jules, as usual brimming with energy, even after a hard match.

'You're right Jules, time to go home. I was just thinking that there are a few things that we can help some others to learn around here.'

'As long as you don't mean the other teams, that's fine by me,' smiled Jules.

Part 2

'You incompetent idiot, what the hell were you doing?' The words were meted out slowly and menacingly, each landed a separate blow with particular emphasis on the words 'incompetent' and 'hell'. It was a melodramatic outburst (the audience being everyone else within the open plan offices) designed to humiliate the recipient as deeply as possible. Paul, the Maintenance Manager, had delivered these words. He looked angry: face flushed, eyes piercing his victim, jaw set firm. In contrast, the sorry individual who was on the receiving end of this attack was a much younger man, a trainee and a new face around the club. He appeared frightened, avoiding eye contact with his tormentor and stuttered a barely audible reply.

'I... I'm sorry, I wasn't sure how to do it.'

It was as if the young man had set a match to a powder keg. Paul's anger exploded into uncontained rage. He had been sitting behind his desk but now he leapt to his feet, lunged forward slamming both palms flat down on the wooden surface and bringing his reddening face a metre closer to his frightened employee. 'Not sure?' he bellowed. Alice could see drops of spittle flying from his lips.

'What the hell do you mean 'not sure', I only showed you last week. How many times do you need showing you useless idiot.'

The trainee winced as if he had been struck; Alice could see his shoulders hunch and his face screw up. There was a whispered 'I'm sorry' immediately followed by Paul's brutal: 'Get out' and then when the trainee didn't immediately leap to his feet and run away Paul shouted again 'Go On Get Out, Get Out Of My Sight'.

Now the trainee was scrambling to his feet and turning away from Paul, Alice could see his face even though his head was bowed; the tears running down his cheeks were unmistakeable.

Alice sidestepped the distressing scene and made her way to Ian's office. This was not a part of the open plan area; instead Ian had a separate office that contained both a desk and an open space with comfortable seating around a coffee table. To the left of the door the desk was placed at right angles to the room, two large displays of green plants softened the atmosphere, but what defined the room was a large curved window that ran the length of the right hand wall facing Ian's desk. It bathed the room in light. From this position, at the very top of the Helen Lunn stand, the window offered an impressive panorama across the stadium.

'Morning Alice, bang on time as usual,' Ian checked his watch and pushed aside the pile of papers that were in front of him.

Alice rarely sat down with Ian, they had quite different roles and when they spoke it was usually by phone or down at the pitch on match days. But today she sat in one of the comfortable chairs to which Ian guided her and took a good look at the club's Managing Director; she saw a tired man. His face looked more lined than she recalled, his skin puffy, he'd put on weight; add to that the state of his desk, in fact the general disorder in his office and he looked like a man under pressure.

'Are you alright Ian?' she asked

'Yes fine,' he smiled brightly, but with a smile that swiftly faded and eyes that gave a different answer. She cocked her head to one side and looked at him quizzically. After an awkward moment of silence he smiled again, this time with a little more life in his expression.

'Ok, maybe not so fine.'

Alice was sorry that she had to put more pressure on Ian; she liked him. He was pleasant, nice to be around, a family man with some great kids and a wife who had always been supportive of Alice even in her early and unproven months as Team Coach for The Mechanics. These days, with the team doing so well, she couldn't put a foot wrong and when she asked for a meeting with Ian, he was swift to agree. Ian also liked her and was mightily relieved that she was doing so well with the team. Right now it was the one bright spot in his working life.

'I am sorry to burden you,' began Alice 'but I am becoming increasingly concerned about what is happening at the club, away from the pitch.'

'So am I Alice,' came Ian's surprising reply. 'If only I could get the rest of our employees to work as well together as the playing team, this club would be transformed. But try as I might I cannot.'

Alice was taken aback by Ian's candour.

'I'm serious,' continued Ian in response to the expression on Alice's face. 'I know this place isn't running right, I need help and if I don't get it I'm going to find myself in trouble. I wondered if you might give me some ideas – you're clearly getting something very right with the players.'

Alice was flattered but unsure how to help. 'Of course I will help if I can Ian, but I'm running a team of players, that's very different to your job.'

'Is it?' replied Ian 'I wonder if that is true. After all, we are talking about getting a group of people to play together as a team. That's exactly what's missing around the club.'

Alice made no reply; she looked as if she was thinking about what he had said, so he continued.

'Give me an example of something that's been concerning you Alice.'

'Ok, but they're all small things.'

'Isn't it the small things that all add up to a big difference?'

'Yes, that's exactly what I say to the players.'

'I know, I've heard you. Come on, an example.'

'All right, the Gamescreens are not all working. The display is fine, but it's not perfect.'

'Yes, good example Alice,' replied Ian 'I noticed them last night as well. Here's the problem that I found this morning. Maintenance should check the screens before every match; they did yesterday morning and found that four screens required work on them. They needed parts, but John who manages the parts department is on holiday, and because none of John's staff have worked with those particular parts before, it took much longer to get hold of the right ones. In fact, they didn't arrive until an hour before the game kicked off. By that time Paul and I were busy in Hospitality with our sponsors for last night, and he had to leave the repair to his trainee. He had shown the trainee how to make that particular repair but the trainee failed to do it. I had Paul in here first thing this morning and told him how let down I felt by his failure to deal with what should be a simple part of his job. I'm waiting for him to come back and explain what happened.'

'Right' said Alice slowly, as she considered the implications of Ian's story. She gazed out of the long window down onto the pitch that had seen so much excitement last night. Today, with empty seats and bathed in sunlight, the stadium looked a very different place. She could see how Ian's reply suggested a lack of teamwork but could she help? As she reached a decision she looked at Ian. 'Perhaps I can help Ian. At least I will do my best.'

Ian looked relieved. 'Great, so how do you do it Alice, how do you get your players to work so well as a team?'

'The first thing I do with any team is to sort out the communication. Everyone must communicate assertively as much of the time as is humanly possible. It's the first step toward getting any group to work as a team.'

'OK I think I've done that. But there is a problem: although they all know how to be assertive, I keep seeing people sliding back to their old ways particularly when they get frustrated.'

'Yes I've just seen an example outside your office...'

'Oh?'

'...Paul being aggressive with one of his people. I suspect from what you've told me it was the trainee who failed to fix the screens last night.'

'I'll speak with Paul,' replied Ian, 'but it's frustration that is causing the problem there. The lad has been shown how to do the job but still didn't do it. I know Paul will regret having lost his temper when he calms down, it's something we have spent a lot of time talking about.'

'OK' said Alice 'so let's accept that you have got your team understanding how to communicate assertively. But you have to keep working at it; it's a tough challenge for some people to change their style and yet so important to team working. After all, what does someone do who is attacked aggressively?'

'Yes I know the answer Alice, they become defensive.'

'And what behaviour does that lead to?'

'They either attack back, or put their defences up and go quiet.'

'and...'

'...and find another route to release their frustration.'

'And their view of the other person?' Alice kept probing.

'It declines and can lead to a bad attitude and non co-operation in the future.'

'So Paul bawling out his trainee can only be harmful for Paul?'

'Yes I agree and I will speak to Paul about that and make it clear to him that it is not acceptable.'

'OK Ian, what about your leadership? That's the other fundamental step – a group must have a good leader if they are to become a team.'

'Yes, I've thought about that, but I've been on several courses and I really do think I get that right. I think carefully about Group Needs and plan to cover them all; I think I put a lot of effort into my leadership. I make sure that each individual is involved and feels treated like an individual, I make sure that everyone understands exactly what is expected of them and their needs around their tasks are met, and I try to help them to work as a team. You can tell me about the personality traits that I display, but I think that I exhibit all the right ones.'

'Yes I agree,' said Alice, 'I think you do as well. But how about your responsibility to make sure that each of your line managers shows leadership in the same way that you have described it?'

'Hmm, that's a bit more difficult.'

'But if you show leadership yet they don't, you are not achieving leadership throughout the organisation, are you?'

Ian's face had relaxed as he became absorbed in the conversation. Now he frowned at Alice, 'You're not going to make this easy for me are you?'

'I'm only trying to help.'

'Yes I know, I appreciate it, but what's the answer? Do I send them all on leadership courses?'

'Sounds a bit long term when you need results now Ian'.

'Yes, but what else can I do?'

'I'm not sure.'

'Well what else do you do Alice?'

'Nothing that I'm really conscious of... well, I coach the team of course, fitness, tactics, game play, but that hardly applies to you. You don't want your people running up and down the training ground do you?'

They both sat staring through Ian's window and out over the stadium. If brain cells made a noise when they worked there would have been a deafening clamour in the office, but since everything was following the laws of nature, silence reigned. Until...

'Hold on Alice. Tell me what you mean by coaching.'

'I mean helping people to learn.'

The two of them looked at each other as they considered these words.

'Actually,' said Alice slowly, 'perhaps this is a key for you as well as me. *Coaching* has a number of effects all of which would help you.'

'That sounds interesting,' replied Ian.

'It *helps get skill levels up.*'

'And some of our problems stem from a lack of skills.'

'Possibly more than you think,' said Alice, 'if you also consider managerial skills. Think about the staff in the parts department who didn't know how to find the right parts or the trainee who didn't know how to fix the screens. You must consider the team leaders to be responsible for this, not the team members.'

'Hold on Alice, I think Paul's trainee is just not up to the job; after all he had been shown how to make the repair.'

'OK, we'll come back to that. But let me add another example of lack of managerial skills: your line managers who need a better understanding of leadership.'

'Now you're challenging me, that last one suggests that I should show them.'

'I think you should, you should coach them, help them to learn. Let me tell you some other *benefits of coaching*: the person being coached feels a greater *respect* for the person coaching them, so when managers coach their staff, respect is being built or reinforced; coaching also *demonstrates good leadership*; coaching is also *a route to motivation* for the coach and the coachee.'

'Sounds like a native Indian tribe.'

'Pardon?'

'Coachees weren't they, you know cowboys and...' Ian's comment tailed away under the nearest thing Alice could make to a withering look. 'OK, Alice, just a passing thought, what were you saying about motivation?'

'People who are being coached find it motivational because it leads them to master new skills or knowledge. It allows them to achieve new things, feel relevant and valued, and that contributes to self-esteem. People who coach are also motivated by helping others to develop, as they see the enthusiasm generated by helping someone to develop and the results achieved by that other person. Where a manager is coaching then the results are observed in terms of better performance by the team.'

'But what about today's example, the trainee who had been coached?'

'Ah, but had he? We need to take a look at how good coaching works. It is not enough just to tell someone something – that does not take into account the way we learn. Most of us forget a large part of what we hear quite quickly. To be a good coach you need to understand how others learn and then adapt your coaching technique to fit that learning method. It may be that Paul just told this trainee how to do this job and didn't effectively coach him.'

Ian stood up and walked to the other side of the office as

he considered Alice's words.

'I think we've hit on something here Alice. Do you?'

'Yes', replied Alice, 'it had never occurred to me before that the coaching skills I use with the team could also be important in other parts of our organisation. The more we consider it, the more it becomes obvious to me that it is essential.'

'I agree. Look, will you help me to understand this Alice? Will you tell me how you coach with the players and then help me work out how to translate those ideas inside the club?'

'Yes, of course if I can help, but I have a busy day today Ian.'

'Me too, can we find some time together tomorrow? I would prefer to meet somewhere else, it might just help some fresh thinking,' he said looking toward the window.

'Why not come to the training ground? You can watch some coaching and then we can talk in the meeting room over there.'

'Sounds like a great idea.'

As Alice left Ian's office and walked back through the open plan area, Paul looked as if he was still brooding on the events of earlier. It made her think that an aggressive confrontation is bad for all concerned.

Part 3

The next morning Alice started her working day at home finishing some paperwork and taking time to consider her plans for the week ahead. She liked to start her days by reflecting on what she intended to achieve, particularly on training days when the team would be discussing and trying new ideas. The responsibilities taken by team members made this relaxed and productive approach possible. Coaching would usually start without her; Jules might run a warm up and perhaps take the defenders through some stick routines whilst The Spider might work with the forwards on fitness levels. Alice was confident that players would be co-operating and coaching each other usefully before she arrived.

Relaxed and ready for her day, she began the short drive across town to the training ground. As she drove she was thinking about how her ideas on coaching could be translated into Ian's environment. It took the tiniest sliver of a second for her senses to register the movement that flashed her focus back to the road. As her eyes took in what she saw her foot was already moving to the brake and slamming down on the pedal. The car lurched into a tyre screeching halt. Her seat belt held her firmly but she flinched as she waited for a second screech from the car behind her to finish and was relieved when no impact followed.

'You idiot' she was yelling at the man who had stepped out onto the road in front of her, knowing that he couldn't hear but nevertheless it made her feel better. She hadn't been driving fast and so managed to stop without hitting him, but the shock had set her pulse pounding.

The man presented a remarkable sight. He was in middle age, medium height with a mass of dark hair and a broad muscular frame. Alice could see this because he was naked above the waist, which given this cool autumn day was bizarre. He didn't look at her, it was as if he hadn't even noticed her or her car. He simply strode ahead (luckily for him there was nothing coming in the opposite direction) and was already disappearing along the other side of the road past a row of shops. Wherever his focus lay it was clearly not on the road or on the people he was passing.

The honk of a car horn startled Alice; she waved an acknowledgement at the driver behind and continued on her journey. For a while the memory of the walking man dominated her thoughts and she kept coming back to his focus and in a way she saw the same focus two nights ago in Jules when she took the penalty. It was as if both of them had removed everything from their thoughts apart from the thing they had chosen to address.

The training ground was a simple place compared to the extravagance of the stadium. Two turf pitches and a single low building that housed a changing area, a gym and a couple of meeting rooms.

Ian was already waiting for Alice when she arrived, and the two made their way to the practice pitches to watch what was going on. They were alive with activity as was usual for a training day with all thirty six players (the squad size specified by The Game League) hard at work on their skills; but today, Alice had pre-arranged for Jules to run a coaching session that would illustrate coaching technique to Ian.

The players were working on a demanding set piece that called for complex movement. It was Jules's latest idea that, if it worked, would fool opposing players into thinking that the ball had been released in a different direction thereby gaining precious moments and allowing an unopposed drive up field. It called for complex, closely timed and unfamiliar manoeuvres, yet within a short time the players seemed to be making good progress.

'Your players seem to pick up new ideas quickly,' said Ian. 'That's so different to the rest of the club where it can take a long time for new skills to develop – take the young technician and the screens as an example.'

'The players learn quickly because they are used to learning (the more you do the easier it gets) and because we help them to learn.'

'Help them to learn?'

'Yes, but to be able to help them you must first *understand how people learn.*'

'OK, that makes sense.'

'The first step is that *they must decide that they want to learn.*' Alice emphasised the point.

'Right, but surely people want to learn things that will help them do their job better?'

'Not necessarily; for example you will find that most people don't react well to surprises. They become unsure and uncertain, a common response is to reject new things that are presented without warning. So *first I give them notice when we are going to learn something new.* Today's coaching session is a good example. Yesterday I discussed the idea of new play strategies with them and told them that I wanted to try some new ideas today. I suggested that they might want to bring some of their own ideas and I gave everyone a chance to ask questions. I made sure that no one had a problem with this. As a result they have arrived today mentally prepared for the coaching. They all want to learn. Imagine if I hadn't done that and they arrived today prepared for a normal day's training and I suddenly say to them I want you to learn some brand new things today.'

'They may have resisted you Alice.'

'Yes, some might have rejected it outright saying things like 'it will never work' or 'we've tried this before', others may have opposed in a less obvious manner, making the learning inexplicably hard work and less productive. But as you can see, they have all got positively involved.'

Ian watched the players who were once again working on the new moves. Every one of them looked focussed on the task, all were contributing ideas and suggestions. There was a sense of involvement and a good humour that seemed to be driving a productive atmosphere. They were trying hard to make Jules's new idea work and appeared to be making real progress. The imaginative move was already fooling Ian's eye as the ball flew between the players.

'So how could you apply that thinking within the club Ian?' Alice was driving the conversation with her questions.

Ian thought for a moment and replied: 'I think that before any coaching takes place, whoever is going to conduct the coaching should give warning to the person being coached. Perhaps they should do as you did, discuss the coaching with them, see if they have any concerns about it and invite their ideas. After all some people might think they don't need coaching or even be afraid that it's part of some plan to show them up or even get rid of them. Does that sound right?'

'Yes, that makes a lot of sense.' Alice nodded her agreement.

'Good, so we've made a start, what happens next?'

'*They must be given the new information in a way that they understand.*'

'Well that's the easy bit then, if you take the trouble to

explain something clearly and slowly you can't go wrong.'

'I'm afraid you can, Ian. Just because you understand does not mean that they do, even if you ask 'do you understand?' and they nod and say 'yes' in response.'

'Hold on Alice, if you explain something clearly and they say they understand, you are saying that they still may not understand?'

'Yes, simply explaining would usually not be good enough and is an ineffective way to coach.'

'Why?' asked a bemused Ian

'Because it takes no account of how our minds work.' Replied Alice 'Did you listen to your car radio on your way here today?'

'Yes'

'What did you hear?'

'A programme about bats.'

'What did it say about bats?'

'Something about caves and breeding.'

'Is that it?'

'It's about what I can remember Alice.'

'How long did you listen?'

'Possibly ten minutes, but I was thinking about other things at the same time.'

'And that's all you remember from ten minutes?'

'Yes, but I didn't know you would be testing me on it, did I?'

'My point is that we forget most of what we hear. We are talking about things that you heard only an hour ago. How much will you remember of those things tomorrow or next week? Telling is not an effective way of teaching.'

'I suppose not when you put it that way. So we have to find more effective ways to get information across to people?'

'Yes and I achieve that by *coaching them using a questioning model and a technique*. My questioning model is called GROW and my technique is to ask as much as possible and tell as little as possible.'

Ian had produced a pad and was busily jotting down notes.

Alice continued '*GROW* stands for Goal, Reality, Options and What will you do next? To be effective with your coaching you must fulfil each of these four stages. Whatever subject you want to help your coachee learn, begin by getting them to paint *a mental picture of the perfect outcome, the Goal.* Consider how you heard Jules begin her coaching just now.'

'Ah yes' said Ian 'she described what her new move would look like if it worked perfectly. She got the players to join in and describe how they would each run and how the ball would travel. So if I were coaching an aggressive person on being assertive we would describe what perfect assertiveness would look like, the words and tone of voice used, the body language displayed. I might describe the behaviour of the other person who, when disciplined assertively, thanked the manager for the help and went away determined not to make the error in question again – the perfect outcome.'

'Nearly, but did you recognise that Jules was using the coaching technique?'

'Asking instead of telling?'

'Yes' she asked the team members what perfect might look like and then questioned them about the answer. She asked them what a perfect pass would look like and let them describe that. She asked how would the ball be travelling? What would you be doing whilst the ball was travelling?'

'Why is questioning important Alice?'

'Because it makes the other person think about the subject. If you just tell them they will forget most of it – maybe because they were thinking about other things, as you were when you partly listened to the programme about bats.

If your radio had come to life and the narrator had started to ask you questions, you would have had to concentrate on what you were hearing so as to be able to answer. Your brain would have to exercise itself around the subject and you would retain much more of what you heard.'

'I see your point; it's obvious when it's explained that way. So in my imaginary coaching session I would not tell my coachee what their Goal looked like, I would get that person to describe it for themself by answering my questions.'

'Correct'

'So I might ask, 'What would you say if you were being assertive? What would your body language be like? How might the other person respond to that?'

'Now you've got the idea Ian, and once you start to work in that way you will find that your questions flow easily and so does their learning. Let's go back to thinking about the players. They described a perfect outcome in fine detail, and then what happened?'

'They had a go, made a complete mess of it and then discussed what had just happened.'

'In detail' added Alice.

'Yes, in detail,' agreed Ian. 'They weren't blaming each other but they discussed exactly what had gone wrong and compared it with their previous discussion of what the perfect move would look like.'

'They were following the GROW model, the *R stands for the Reality, a precise picture of what is happening at the moment.* Having completed these two stages you have a valuable comparison – the Goal with present Reality. What is important here is that you can see *the gap between the two.*'

Ian was scribbling notes on his pad 'Goal and Reality' he repeated 'I see that and I use the asking method to get them to describe the Reality?'

'Yes and you may need to be strong with your questions because sometimes people don't want to admit just how bad things have been, or they may not even realise how bad things have been.'

'So in my coaching session on assertiveness I would achieve the R in GROW by getting the aggressive person to describe their own aggressive behaviour. I would ask them to describe what it looked and sounded like and what the likely outcomes would be in terms of the behaviour of the other person.'

'Yes, although you may have to help them, you won't get everything you want through questions; the guideline is tell only as little as you must and ask as much as possible.'

'So that's the Goal and Reality of GROW. What did you say the O was?'

Before Alice could answer a rumbling explosion came from somewhere beyond the perimeter fence. Ian puffed out his cheeks and exhaled loudly, the colour drained from his face and he staggered to one side. The yells and shouts from the pitch immediately hushed and Jules shouted: 'Sorry Ian are you alright?' Ian raised an unsteady arm and weakly waved an acknowledgement while Alice picked up the ball that was rolling gently at Ian's feet and threw it back onto the pitch.

'Perhaps, if we're not going to keep our eye on the ball we should go back into the meeting room to finish this discussion,' said Alice. Ian nodded slowly regaining his breath and hobbled carefully alongside Alice away from the pitch.

Part 4

In the comfort and quiet of the meeting room the two sat together. Ian cradled a strong mug of coffee as Alice continued with her explanation of GROW.

'The *O* in GROW stands for *Options, which means the options you have for closing the gap between your Goal and your Reality*,' said Alice. 'In other words what is the plan? This is where you discuss the solution. It may be that you have some knowledge that they don't, the guideline is still – tell only as little as you must and ask as much as possible. Can you help them to work out the answer?'

'So back to Jules and the other players,' said Ian, 'they were discussing how to make the new idea work, trying alternative approaches and deciding who would play what part. They were looking carefully at what had gone wrong in their first attempt and working out how to get it right.'

'And what about your example of assertiveness coaching Ian?'

'I would ask the coachee for ideas about what they might say differently or how they would amend their body language, throwing in my own suggestions if necessary.'

'Yes, and you continue that process until you have a workable plan. Then comes the *W* of GROW, *What will you do? It means to make sure that whatever has been agreed is put into action.* The 'What will you do?' part of the GROW model ensures that the learner practises. Without this we would have agreed some theory without any guarantee of it being put into action. With the players, the W part of today's work might be achieved by agreeing a practise routine over a period of days or even weeks and they know that I will be checking what they were doing. To understand this, let's consider again how people learn. If I explain a new move to a player, they might understand it but they cannot yet do it.'

'No of course not,' replied Ian, 'they would have to practise, so practice is an important part of the learning process.'

'Yes a vital part. As a coach I have to get the other person to both understand and to *practise*. Whilst they are practising I need to *re-enforce the learning*, remind them of it and keep their understanding accurate, and I have to *encourage* them'.

'Encourage them?' asked Ian

'Yes, we all benefit from encouragement. Can you give me an example of something that you have been learning?'

'Will golf do? I've been learning for months but I'm still not very good.'

'Can you hit a ball cleanly from the tee?'

'Usually.'

'Could you when you first started to play?'

'No, I won't forget that. A friend took me to a practise driving range. I had never played before, and remember swinging at several balls that just spun off sideways.'

'How did you feel?'

'Embarrassed. And then when it happened a few times more I can remember getting annoyed and frustrated.' Ian looked awkward and embarrassed as he relived these events in his mind.

'These are typical of the negative emotions that we experience when we practise with something that is new to us,' said Alice. 'They often lead to a fear that we will never be able to do the new thing. That's why you hear learners saying things like 'I'm not cut out for this' early in the learning process, and it is why so many of us give up learning new things before we have mastered them. So why did you keep playing golf?'

'I really wanted to learn. I thought it would be good for my career; a lot of business people I know play and I know a lot of business gets done on the golf course. I was lucky, my friend was supportive and took the trouble to take me a few times whilst I learned the basics.'

'So you really wanted to learn?'

'Yes.'

'That was the first stage in place and your friend helped you learn, he encouraged and coached you as you were practising.'

'Yes, I suppose he did,' replied Ian.

'So as a result you persevered and began to build a new skill.'

'I see your point, so when I've completed my coaching I must make sure that whoever I'm coaching sets some sort of action plan to practise. After my assertiveness coaching my manager must have a plan to practise and I must keep an eye on him to see that it is being put into practise. Perhaps I ask him to check back with me and tell me what has been happening.'

'You've got it, Ian. Would you like to summarise what we have been saying?'

'Yes, we must first understand how people learn before we can help them to learn. As a coach we must take these things into account if we want to make learning stick. We have said that: *we must make sure that the other person wants to learn; they must receive new information in a way that they understand; they must practise with the new knowledge and that knowledge must be reinforced and encouragement given during a period of practise*. Only if those things are achieved will the other person develop a new skill.'

'That's great and how do we make all that happen?' asked Alice.

'We discuss coaching with the coachee before the session takes place and then we coach using the GROW model and by asking instead of telling.'

'That's exactly it Ian. As we have been discussing this I have realised that the methods I use with players need no adaptation at all for you to use around the rest of the club. I'd never thought about it like that before.'

'I agree Alice and I can immediately see why a lack of coaching has caused some real difficulties. Take the problem we discussed yesterday, the four screens that didn't get fixed before last night's match. If the people that I mentioned – John the Parts Manager and his staff, Paul the Maintenance Manager and his trainee – had been working together as a team, none of that would have happened. John would have coached his staff so that they knew how to get the parts and Paul's trainee would have known how to make the repair. I also realise that these events are my responsibility. I must be the head coach in this organisation and I must set the standard and lead by example.'

'Now I'm learning,' said Alice. 'I only ever saw coaching as a way to get players to play to the best of their ability. What you are showing me is that coaching is essential to team working in any organisation.'

'This has been a revelation Alice. I can see in coaching the solution to many of the problems that we are facing. I'm going to go back to the office and make a plan to develop a coaching habit throughout the club, and I'm going to start by helping Paul understand how to discipline and coach his people.'

'Do you think coaching will solve your problems?' asked Alice.

'I'm sure it will make a huge difference,' replied Ian. 'If it can help me get assertive communication established and maintained throughout the club, and I continue to show good leadership, surely we must be well on the way to building a real team.'

'That's how it has worked with the players.'

'I can't help feeling that there may be some other things to learn but just now, for the first time in months, I'm looking forward to going back to my office.'

At that moment the door burst open; it was Jules. 'Sorry to interrupt boss but we've finished for this morning and everyone's ready to go, is that OK?'

'Yes Jules...' Alice abruptly stopped talking as she looked up at Jules, 'What is that on your forehead?'

Jules had a perfectly round purple circle on her forehead and two others on her sweatshirt.

'I think someone's being playing a joke on us,' replied Jules. 'These purple bubbles came floating over the fence when we were on the training pitch and I jumped up and headed one. But it won't wash off!'

'You know that could start a whole new trend Jules. All those youngsters who think you're wonderful are going to want one after tonight's match,' replied Alice, failing to restrain a smile.

'Great marketing opportunity,' said Ian still nursing his dented pride. 'Perhaps we could do a line of stick-on purple transfers to sell in the team shop.'

'Thanks for your support,' said Jules with her indestructible grin firmly in place but heading off home to start scrubbing her forehead.

Learning Questions

1.   How had Paul the maintenance manager unwittingly

caused the problem with the screens?

2. How does Paul's confrontation with the trainee show a link between this chapter and chapter 3?

3. How could the parts department manager have avoided the problem occurring?

4. Why had Ian forgotten most of the radio programme about bats?

5. What is likely to happen without the W in GROW?

Learning Summary – Coaching

- Coaching is about helping others to learn
- In a team, where skill levels are rising so is confidence
- A good coach earns the respect of the coachee, and so leaders should be good coaches
- Understanding how we learn helps you deliver effective coaching
- It is important to address the others persons attitude before starting coaching
- The GROW model is a valuable structure for a coaching session
- Using well formed questions is better than telling - one important step when preparing to coach is to think of some good coaching questions

6

A Significant Day
(A Key to Motivation)

Part 1

A MARTIAN ATE MY GRANNY screamed the newspaper headline; MARTIAN EATS GRANNY agreed the billboard.

'Ayooomybya iiigryer.'

Had Eric come face to face with the infamous Martian? No. He reminded himself not to entertain flights of fancy since, as a Journalist, he must stick to accurate facts.

'Ayooomybya iiigryer.'

'Alright Tom?' Eric issued the questioning greeting to the newspaper seller, catching him pausing for breath between expletives.

Tom was a memorable and venerable old gentleman. One would use the term 'old' advisedly since this was merely an impression; it would be difficult to pin down Tom's precise age by observation alone. His straggle of shoulder length grey hair struck creative angles depending on the prevailing weather conditions, and a pair of glasses with large round black plastic frames made a strong horizontal signature across his weather beaten face. But it was Tom's smile that Eric found most engaging; it pounced on you without warning. His face was otherwise set in what seemed to be a permanent scowl, and then if something happened to please Tom you would be ambushed by the smile. His lips would rip up at the corners, pushing his eyes into twinkling life, but the smile was made memorable by the absence of most of his teeth, except the three or four hardy survivors (Eric had never got close enough to make a precise count) who seemed determined to impress by wearing smart black or brown outfits and lounging at jaunty angles in Tom's mouth.

Eric liked talking to people. He had a desire to find out who they were and had long ago learned that when people remain anonymous they have nothing to offer. Instead, explore them and you find that everyone has a story to tell, a personality to offer, some potential lying dormant. Eric had begun to chat to Tom, who he passed several times each day on his route to and from the office. He soon discovered that 'the funny old guy who sold the papers' was a character of real depth. As a young man Tom had been a soldier, had seen combat and been decorated for actions he now refused to discuss. When he left the army he spent time in the Far East running a business, there he had married a local girl and they had had a son. A tragic accident robbed him of both and he ultimately returned, forever changed by the sadness and the shock of what had happened. Tom was an intelligent man who made his own accommodation with life, which he now lived in a simple if eccentric manner.

When Eric had asked Tom if he could help him with the weekly Nostalgia column it was a desperate lunge at the first elderly person he met who might be able to remember past times in The Town. He held little hope that this shell of a man would come good, but was pleasantly surprised by the outcome. It soon became clear that if Tom didn't know something about The Town's history, he could find someone who did, and he attacked the task with enthusiasm. In truth the Nostalgia column for which Eric had received accolades was rich in variety and accuracy because Tom and his friends (and friends of friends) wrote most of it. Not that Eric pretended otherwise – he always attributed his voluntary contributors. He would receive a particularly hectic smile from Tom when the words 'with thanks to Tom Arnold' had appeared in the column on the previous day.

'Got a great un for you boy,' said Tom, waving a folded copy of the *Crier* in Eric's direction. 'A real special un.'

'Fantastic Tom! I can always rely on you. Will you come in later?'

'I will, boy. It's a real special un,' added Tom with a wink that appeared to involve every muscle in his face.

Having recently achieved the age of forty, Eric had attained the stage in life where the implication of youth in the address 'boy' was a pleasure rather than an insult. He smiled back at Tom. 'See you later.'

'Ayooomybya iiigryer,' bellowed Tom, as Eric pushed his way around the revolving door that afforded entry to the reception of *The Town Crier* offices and sealed the interior from the din of Tom's Martian cry.

The pile of newspapers that Tom had remaining for sale encouraged Eric; it had for several years been Eric's reliable guide to daily sales. Since sales were such a focus at the moment, he was pleased to see that the pile was low for this time in the afternoon – the Martian headline must be working.

Eric was a News Editor on the paper, having previously been a reporter with a competitor. He enjoyed his work, but like most of his colleagues was finding the pressure of recent months increasingly uncomfortable.

Glo ('don't call me Gloria') Dean was the Editor and had been for the past five years. Glo was efficient. Always smartly dressed in a tweedy way, she buzzed – a busy bee at all times.

Glo was a gifted communicator who appeared to know every member of staff by first name. Eric had never heard her lose her temper; instead he had been on the receiving end of one of her stern lectures that made you feel very guilty and determined not to make the same mistake again. It would be safe to say that Glo was assertive and that she made sure that she led an assertive team. She was always swift to correct passive or aggressive behaviour amongst her staff. The only time she ever got noticeably annoyed was when someone called her Gloria (which she hated, demanding at all times to be addressed as Glo), and that was when the famous 'Don't call me Gloria' would echo around the office. It had thus become tradition that any new starters were sent unwittingly to deliver a message to her and advised to address her as Gloria. A round of applause would greet the inevitable expletive from Glo, who by now went along with the ritual in good spirit. In short, everybody liked her, and she was particularly popular amongst the journalists and print shop workers. But with her management team it was a love-hate relationship. Despite Glo's hard work and attractive personality there remained a constant tension between them, for Glo had her frustrating traits that were not apparent to most but to her managers could be infuriating.

Glo was a workaholic. Frequently first in and last out of the building; she clearly loved her job and took the newspaper's successes and failures personally. She held an interest in everything that happened. Glo had been Business Editor before her promotion and retained some of those responsibilities, maintaining influential contacts and still attending meetings alongside Alun the new Business Editor. To Alun this was a cause of irritation, but he had to admit that Glo had valuable contacts that he did not. Further, Glo's experience was extensive and had delivered several strong stories for *The Crier* before the nationals had got to them.

But despite the long hours that Glo worked, it would be common for managers to be waiting for Glo to complete a task or make a decision. Since Glo involved herself in so much, many felt that they must seek frequent guidance from her, thus their own decisions were delayed and those seeking her confirmation or advice constantly interrupted her.

This is what Glo thought:

I am an assertive leader, I am not aggressive or passive and I try to make sure that my people are assertive, although I think I often fail in getting them to be assertive with me. I don't think that they always tell me what they think.

I try to lead by fulfilling all three areas of group needs. I think I do well with Team and Task needs, but I find some Individual needs are difficult in practise. For example, I try to get to know all my staff, involve them and help them develop, but that is not an easy thing to achieve. I have attempted to give them some of my tasks, but in most cases I end up having to take over again or redo the task myself when what they do isn't good enough. They just don't have the experience. Otherwise, I am confident that I show the right personality traits. I think I perform well as a leader.

I encourage coaching amongst them and have sent several of my people on coaching courses. I do see that this makes a difference and that some of my managers are developing their team members as a result.

What frustrates me is that, despite all this, they still don't really work as a team. Is it them, are they just not of the right calibre? Or perhaps I am asking an impossible task in such a diverse organisation.

From Glo's perspective she saw herself as the indispensable centre of the organisation. From the perspective of her team she seemed equally indispensable since they needed the skills and contacts that she possessed and that they did not. And so a tension grew without anyone really knowing why. The tension grew within Glo because, despite her best efforts and long working hours, her managers did not seem to be able to deliver the results that she required. The tension grew amongst her managers because they all experienced the frustration of being dependant on Glo. They needed her but resented it; they were helped by her but must ask and wait for that help. Since Glo was so skilled at communication, and was a thoughtful and considerate person, she won the hearts and minds of those she did not directly manage and set her managers on an uncomfortable knife edge – loving her and hating her. The net result was a mysteriously dysfunctional 'team'.

As a result their newspaper was struggling. Just five years ago *The Town Crier* had been purchased by almost fifteen percent of the local adult population, and yet today this figure hovered at just above ten percent and was on a declining trend that could soon take it below this emotive marker. The newspapers owners were concerned and they were looking to Glo for answers.

Earlier in the day Eric had attended the editorial meeting. This meeting had assumed an extra importance in recent weeks as the pressure on the team increased. Glo now insisted that all Sub Editors attend each day, and she had underlined over and again the plan for rebuilding circulation – 'revive to survive' had become her battle cry. Deliver quality and depth, interest and a great read; use the headline stories to bring the readers back. Once they sample the newly invigorated newspaper they will continue to buy and circulation will rise.

That was the plan defined by Glo.

Eric liked his colleagues but could see that they didn't really work together as a team. For example Joe produced an excellent sports section but he delivered it with little regard for anyone else. Eric didn't see people helping and supporting each other; he saw each completing their own tasks. Neither did he see initiative and flair, or for that matter real enthusiasm, not in the way that he saw it in Tom's Nostalgia team. Was he expecting too much? Perhaps in a working environment where people have worked together for many years this is the way it had to be. Was it the fate of the regional press to decline in an age where there was greater media rivalry and greater competition for people's leisure time? Alongside these thoughts he reached a further conclusion that made him uncomfortable: that they were producing a mediocre newspaper. It was alright, it wasn't bad, but it did not excel or excite.

'Wakey, wakey boy!'

Eric hadn't noticed the approach of Tom, which was extraordinary since Tom was not an easy character to miss. This was because he dressed to kill. It was as if a colour blind family of assorted shapes and sizes had donated their wardrobe to Tom and he simply took a lucky dip into it each day. Today he was wearing a navy blue anorak with large furry hood several sizes too large for him; consequently his hands disappeared into the sleeves and the garment hung and swung as he moved. He wore this over a purple sweater with a fraying neck from which a green shirt collar protruded. This eye catching outfit was augmented by red cord trousers whose legs ended approximately six inches above pristine white trainers and a pair of socks that had surely never been considered a pair before that day, given their conflicting colours and materials. Add to this picture a limp that made

Tom lunge alarmingly from side to side as he walked and we must conclude that Eric had been deeply engrossed in thought not to be aware of Tom approaching his desk. That's why he jumped when Tom addressed him.

'I told you I got a special 'un,' continued Tom, his enthusiasm apparent.

'Come on then Tom, sit down and lets take a look. We need some real news around here.'

That morning's editorial meeting had been faced with a no-news-day and in desperation decided to go for the Martian Eats Granny story. It was an idea of Eric's not initially meant seriously. A boy from the local school was about to have a book published with the title *A Martian Ate My Granny*. The publication of the book was a true story, the Martian Eats Granny was part of the schoolboy's fantasy storyline. The publishers of the book had happily agreed that *The Crier* could use the sleeve cover picture, showing a strangely shaped creature emerging from a shiny disc spacecraft, as a front page photograph. The article was written in such a way that it would take you to the second paragraph to find that an extra terrestrial had not actually consumed a granny in The Town.

'Is that honest?' A young journalist had asked Eric.

'It's journalism,' had come the non-committal reply.

It looked to Eric, from the evidence of Tom's rapidly reducing pile of newspapers, as if the gamble of resorting to journalism had paid off. Well for today anyway.

Part 2

'Morning everyone. Thank you for being prompt. Great result yesterday – now lets make sure we keep the momentum going.'

The editorial meeting convened every morning and Glo would lead the discussion about the day's stories, making a first decision about a headline.

The *Town Crier* offices had an old fashioned feel to them. This was particularly true of the oak panelled meeting room with its centrepiece polished mahogany table, a relic of a previous era when the newspaper was privately owned. Today it was part of TAMedia International, a media conglomerate owning publications in several countries. Around the table sat Joe Strong, the Sports Editor, Eric and his counterpart Dan, both News Editors, Alun the Business Editor, Sue the Features Editor and the unusual Freda who had been the newspaper's crossword compiler for almost twenty years; Freda's presence at these meetings was a habit that remained from the days of Glo's predecessor.

'So what have we got for today?' Glo surveyed the assembled faces.

'It's The Factory demolition today, Glo,' said Dan. 'Should be some good pictures – it's a story that touches lots of people in The Town.'

'I agree Dan, that could be a strong lead. I'll get onto BleakCorp, a corporate angle will add some depth.' Dan's face showed a flicker of irritation, which Glo did not notice.

'Anything else?' Glo looked around at the others and frowned when nothing was forthcoming.

'The Mechanics are playing again tonight,' ventured Joe

'but that's no big story they'll win as usual.'

'I've got some good back-up on The Factory story,' said Eric, 'my researchers...' laughter around the room

'You mean your Dad's Army,' Joe interrupted.

'...my researchers,' persevered Eric, taking the ribbing in good humour, 'for the Nostalgia column have found out that today is a day of historic coincidences. This day twenty years ago The Factory was sold to BleakCorp, and this day thirty years ago the David Mars statue in the park was unveiled.'

'Oh, the one with him holding that machine,' said Dan.

'Yes, anyone know what sort of machine it is?'

Blank faces provided the answer to Eric's question.

'It's a set of five cogs meshed together.' Eric was using his hands to aid his explanation. 'One in the centre and the other four arranged around the outside. It represents a human mechanism. It was David Mars's way of showing how people work together. The central cog represents the leader and the whole mechanism shows the influence the leader has on the team and the influence they have on each other. That's why there's an inscription at the base of the statue that says 'Helping people to do a better job'.'

'Nice touch to the story Eric,' Glo looked impressed.

'Well, there's more: its sixty years to the day since the old library was opened – says so on a plaque on the wall outside.'

'OK Eric, respect is due,' said Joe.

'All down to my Dad's Army Joe.' The two returned smiles; whilst they regularly sparred like this there was an underlying friendship and mutual respect between them.

Glo stood, picking up her notepad. 'Great. Looks like we know where we're going today. Get some great pictures and let's sell some papers. Anything else?'

'My next door neighbour's shed got burned down by an intruder last night.' Freda was leaning forward and peering over her glasses. Since Freda was always treated with a respectful courtesy it was left to Glo to tactfully tell her that this did not rate front-page news in the newly invigorated *Town Crier.*

'You look fed up,' said Eric as he and Dan walked back to their office.

'Why does she get to call BleakCorp? It's as if I can't be trusted to do the whole story myself.'

'Doesn't she know the BleakCorp chairman?'

'Yes, she seems to know everyone.'

'So isn't she the best person to do it?'

'Yes I suppose so, but it's still frustrating.'

With the meeting closed, it was Dan who was detailed to go to The Factory and report on the demolition. Eric had been so drawn in to the history of David Mars through his discussion with Tom that, despite the time pressures he was under, he also decided to go and watch.

When he arrived at The Factory gates a crowd had already gathered. They were a mix of young people there for the excitement and novelty of seeing a large building raised to the ground, and older people who looked sad rather than excited and had come to see a piece of their history destroyed. Eric knew the policeman who was keeping the crowd outside the gates.

'Your guys are already through there,' said the policeman pointing to a group of four who were standing behind a neatly placed row of bollards 'and it's a hard hat beyond this point.'

Donning a white hard hat from a small pile just inside the gateway, Eric walked across to the group: two men in overalls who were clearly part of the demolition team, Dan and the photographer. Dan was in the process of identifying everyone present and noting relevant information carefully on a pad.

There was a murmur from the crowd and Eric looked up to see someone emerging from the building in front of them and striding across the car park toward the gate. Eric saw a big man with a shock of dark hair; as he came closer tears could be seen running down his face. One of the men in overalls shouted: 'Put your hat on Jack, health and safety,' but the man was staring fixedly ahead and seemed not to hear or even notice their presence. He strode past them and toward the gates. The photographer raised his camera and captured the scene. Eric and the others were transfixed and turned to watch him go, and then as he passed through the gates the man tore off his shirt and flung it on the ground, which seemed to Eric an act of blind and bitter frustration. The crowd parted and the policeman who clearly knew the man said 'Come on Jack,' more, it seemed to Eric, as a comfort than an admonishment as the big man swept by and disappeared from view.

'Been here all his working life,' said one of the men in overalls in simple explanation.

It was to be another half hour before the building was ready to go but Eric was determined to wait and see the final act. Jack's distress had made a real impression on Eric and his discussion with Tom about David Mars and his methods had pricked his interest in this piece of The Town's history. His thoughts also turned to what was happening at the *Town Crier*. Suddenly he knew what was wrong. It's all about delegation, he thought. That's at the heart of why people are not working as a team.

And he knew this because of his experience in a very different environment.

Part 3

Eric worked voluntarily for a youth group, and had done for many years. The group was well established, run by a team of committed helpers. Some of these were parents of children that attended the group; others helped because they had gained by being members of the group in their own youth, and now wanted to give something back.

Each year Eric told himself that he didn't have time to do this, his career was too demanding or he should spend more time with his family, but then his own children started to benefit from the youth group and somehow he just stayed.

What thrust these thoughts to the forefront of his mind was the jolt that Jack's image had given him, which somehow brought several threads of thinking together to form an irresistibly bigger picture. He saw Glo's inability to get everyone at the *Town Crier* working together as a team, despite apparently doing many things well as a manager; this contrasted with David Mars's obvious success at doing so, and the inscription on his statue 'Helping people to do a better job'; and those thoughts brought him to JB.

JB was the youth group leader and had been since Eric was a boy. Everyone involved in the organisation used his initials instead of his full name; it was a sign of the general acceptance of his leadership. His style was typified by the way he seemed to do little himself but instead get others to do for him. The casual observer might mistake this for laziness, but in fact it was inspired people management. JB was an expert delegater, and this was how he managed to involve and motivate unpaid volunteers to give so fully of their time and energy. As these ideas developed in Eric's mind, the dramatic contrast between Glo and JB became apparent. JB did little and got things done, Glo did too much and didn't allow people to do enough. JB had once advised Eric on this: 'people who are dependant on you will not respect you, they will resent you,' and that, thought Eric, was exactly what was happening at the *Town Crier*.

What struck Eric about this comparison was that JB had to get the commitment of people to work as a team without the inducement of payment. There was no public funding for youth workers; it was a labour of love. Yet Glo, with some substantial salaries at her disposal, was unable to get results from her people. At the youth group, team working was endemic; people constantly helped each other to achieve common goals. Between them they had raised funds to build a new meeting hall, run trips and camps, organised a wide range of activities and got the kids involved wherever possible in making things happen. But Eric could see clearly that JB delegated every task that he possibly could, and in doing so he made a better organisation. Like David Mars, he was helping people to do a better job.

These were the conclusions that Eric had drawn about Delegating: A leader must *delegate* as much as possible in order to *develop people*. If people are not developing they will become disillusioned and unhappy, their confidence may decline and they will begin to appear less able. A leader should approach all of his or her team as if that leader is *training a successor*. Eric had never seen a leader train a successor and then be unwillingly replaced by that person, but he had seen leaders who failed to train a successor and then could not be promoted. If leaders coached their people with the aim of getting them to be able to do everything that the leader could, then those people would be better able to do their own tasks. They would better understand the implications of their own job for the team and therefore act with more consideration for others and, when necessary, they could stand in for the leader. Hence the much quoted test of a good manager that 'all runs smoothly when they are away' is completely true.

Delegation *motivates* people by helping them build self-esteem. It enables them to achieve more; allowing them to feel more confident in their abilities and so making them feel valued. A further reason to delegate is that it frequently *gets the job done to a better standard*. In Glo's case, Eric had no doubt that because she involved herself in so many things, some of those things were not done to the best possible standard. She stretched herself too far. People to whom tasks are delegated often put more thought and effort into those tasks because they are novel and new to them, and because they want to impress.

A final reason to delegate is simply to *increase the productivity of the team*. The more people who can accomplish key tasks then the more will get done, but when key tasks can only be carried out by a few, the team will inevitably spend time waiting for those people.

Again Eric recalled some advice from JB. He had said that you must delegate, but that many who tried to delegate did it ineffectively and so failed. They got frustrated because people didn't understand or learn the task quickly and then grabbed it back from them, thinking 'if you want a job done properly you must do it yourself'. JB had warned Eric that when you delegate you must experience the discomfort of watching someone do something to a lower standard than you would do it yourself. He advised recalling when you first learnt the task yourself: were you as good as you are now? Of course not, you were probably like the person that you are trying to delegate to, you would never have learnt if that task had been taken away from you.

It seemed plain to Eric that the skills of *coaching and delegating are closely interlinked*. You need to coach to be able to delegate.

What defeated many leaders was not knowing how to delegate and as a consequence delegating ineffectively. Luckily for Eric, JB had given him some clear pointers on this.

Start by *selling the task*, convince them why they should do it. To do this, *put yourself in their shoes* and identify the benefit for that other person. Explaining how it fits their future can be an effective way of doing this – for example you could say: 'I want you to understand as much of my job as possible. It will help you to develop in your own role and will mean that I can rely on you when I am not here'. You must have a *crystal clear vision* of the task and outcome that you wish to delegate, and *explain why it must be done*. You must then *communicate clearly* to get that same vision into the mind of the other person. This is like coaching – describe to them what perfect looks like, then show how and *follow the coaching process*. Remember to use questions to help the other person understand, rather than just telling them. Having done that you must now make sure that they do it. Set a *realistic timetable* and perhaps *a finish date for the task,* and you might also agree regular *review and feedback* if the task is going to take a period of time. On completion, always *evaluate the other person's performance* with them by comparing the outcome with the original vision. This is important, since you are helping the other person to develop. Remember to *reward and encourage* as appropriate, and be aware that meaningful praise can be ample reward.

Proof to Eric of the validity of all this was JB's success in bringing volunteers enthusiastically together over many years. Eric thought also of his own success with the Nostalgia team. He had delegated most of the news gathering function to this growing group, and they attacked it with enthusiasm. Once Eric had recognised Tom's interest he had followed JB's guidelines, adapting them to the circumstances. The result was a constant flow of high quality material from some highly motivated individuals.

Seeing the *Town Crier* through this filter, he saw that, although Glo tried hard to fulfil every element that was necessary for a leader to create a great team, she did not delegate and so she did not have a team; instead she had a group of people working below their potential. Because she got some things right she achieved mediocrity rather than disaster. Eric was resolving to talk to Glo about this when the siren wailed to warn that the detonation was imminent.

He moved back behind the line of bollards. The photographer raised his camera and Dan waited expectantly, notebook in hand.

A dull 'whumpf' came from within the building; it hit the stomach with more strength than it hit the ear. At first nothing seemed to happen and then a rumble followed that grew as the base of the building appeared to dissolve around its entire perimeter. The roofline kinked and then began to sink slowly like a stunned boxer, whose body, having taken a brief moment to absorb a knockout blow, slides helplessly to the ground. The rumble became a roar as the pace of the building's disintegration accelerated. A widening skirt of smoke and dust grew outward from its base as the centre fell inward in slow motion.

The photographer's camera was clicking furiously, recording each stage of the dramatic process. Eric was surprised by the emotion that welled up inside him as The

Factory entered its final death throes. The place gave one final roar as the last standing parts hit the ground and then came a peculiar silence in which only the dust cloud moved... and it moved toward them! Suddenly the foreman shouted 'Down, get down,' and dived forward onto the ground. The rest of the group followed his example and Eric pressed his face into the car park gravel, screwing his eyes tightly shut as the cloud reached and rushed over them, expecting at any moment blows to head and body from flying masonry. But none came.

As the dust settled it became obvious that the cloud of debris had lost momentum some way before them, and what had reached them had been only a light dust whipped up by a sudden breeze. Eric raised his head and looked across at Dan – they both laughed as they looked at each other, each seeing a dusty vagrant. As they eased themselves to their feet they were surprised one last time by a final grinding crunch from the rubble before them, as if something inside the felled building was eventually succumbing under the immense weight of fallen stone. Oddly the sound was not unlike a deep dark laugh. The last laugh. To Eric's ear it sounded defiant.

Part 4

Eric sat back, enjoying the comfort and authority that came with the large leather executive chair, feeling a mix of excitement and trepidation on his first day as Editor of the *Town Crier*. Two days had passed since he had thrown himself flat on his face in the car park of the demolished factory building.

On the morning following those events the usual editorial meeting had been convened. It had begun in congratulatory manner; The Factory story had delivered sales. Dan had done a great job pulling the threads together into several pages of high quality material – excellent pictures, interviews with ex workers in the crowd, the information that Glo had gathered from BleakCorp – and then he had taken the information that Eric's nostalgia team had unearthed and woven it into the main article to excellent effect. It had impressed everyone and shown Dan's potential as a first class journalist.

But the mood of optimism soon dissolved as the predictable hunt began for the headline of the day. This desperate focus of Glo's had come to hang over everyone, and build a tension before the discussion even began. No one had anything that Glo would accept as a headline and in truth it appeared from the contributions that there was nothing.

This is what those who sat around the meeting table thought:

Joe the Sports Editor thought: I don't really care about the front page. I have a full sports section. I offered my back page headline for the front page and she has dismissed it again... The Mechanics could win the league this year, that really would be a front page story.

Dan thought: I heard some things yesterday that make me think there might be a story about BleakCorp but I'm not going to let Glo get her teeth into it. If I mention it, she will only snatch it as usual. I will keep quiet about it and do my own work on it today. Maybe I can deliver it tomorrow as a finished story.

Sue the Features Editor thought: This is nothing to do with Features. I will keep smiling and look helpful, but I really wish I didn't have to attend these meetings. We have so much to do today; we're under pressure to finish the piece on fashion models for tonight's edition.

Alun the Business Editor thought: I want the sort of praise that Dan has just received. He did a great job but I never get the chance, Glo always seems to get involved if it's something big. I have heard a whisper that there is some kind of financial scandal about to break at BleakCorp and I've got a friend calling me back later to tell me more. It could make a nice article. Anyhow why should I be bothered about the front page, that's down to Eric and Dan. I'm still going to have a job even if one of them bites the dust.

Freda the crossword compiler thought: remove the physical education from the landscape to cause a shake up – that's it, the last clue finished, crossword 1040 completed.

Glo thought: I'm at my wits end. This endless pressure to come up with winning stories is exhausting me and so is the lack of enthusiasm or initiative from these people. I've led them well and encouraged them, but they just don't have what it takes. There are going to have to be some changes around here.

Eric thought: This is getting worse by the day. Not only are we

> failing to work as a team but also the motivation of everyone around this table is falling away.

Once again Eric made the mental comparison between this group of people and those he worked alongside each week at the youth group. He considered the difference in their levels of motivation. *Motivation* is what makes you want to do something, he thought; it is a drive that comes from within. One person cannot directly control the motivation of another but can strongly influence it by putting someone in a situation from which they are likely to find motivation.

Eric reflected that the fundamental concept about motivation is that *people are only motivated by something they do not have*, in other words attaining something that has been a motivator means that this thing will cease to motivate. The workers who work hard for a bonus are no longer motivated by that bonus after they have achieved it; the hungry person will make an effort to get food but once they have eaten and appetite is satiated the drive to get food is gone until the hunger returns; a workforce is not motivated by having a smart new office, only by the prospect of having a smart new office. Once a move has been made from old premises to new, and the novelty has worn off, the new office is not a source of motivation. Herein lies the challenge of motivation with material things; the motivation is limited by the satisfaction of the desire.

It is common to hear people confusing themselves on the subject of motivation, thought Eric, by repeating the wishful thinking 'all people are different'. At a motivational level this is not true: people are generally the same in that most of us are motivated by exactly the same fundamental needs, and a need is something that powerfully drives behaviour even when the driven person is not aware of what their mind is doing to them.

As a student, Eric remembered popular theories of motivation being explained to him. In the classroom they seemed irrelevant to the real world and for many years remained to him no more than lines written in workbooks. Later in his working life he recalled these same theories paraded again on training courses and meaning no more than they had done years before. Only when JB explained motivation to him in the context of real people did it become clear. The simplicity was stunning and made Eric think that those people who had lectured him on the subject over the years did not really understand it themselves, but were simply repeating theories from books for the purpose of completing exams and getting certificates.

JB's explanation was that almost all people were motivated by *five needs* and that the first three of those needs usually followed an order in which one must be satisfied before the other becomes a need.

The *first need is to survive* closely followed by the *second need, to be safe*. This means that if a human being feels threatened, then their actions, driven by their motivation, will be to do everything they can to save themselves and then, having achieved survival, will do everything they can to achieve a position of safety. Normally in the working environment these needs are satisfied since an employee has a home, job and income, but should these things become threatened e.g. the person falls into heavy debt which threatens their home, their motivation and focus will return to achieving survival and safety. To motivate someone in this position you offer him or her things that will help to achieve what they need. You must also be aware that helping someone to survive and be safe may earn you some loyalty but does not ensure any level of motivation. That is because once those needs are settled then the *third need, to belong*, takes over as the prime motivator.

Needing to belong means needing to fit in and be accepted. The very circumstance of being recognised and known, and having relevance, is the meaning of this need. Anyone who has been unemployed might recognise the power of this need, having experienced the emptiness left by not belonging. For people who are self employed, being recognised and welcomed at the workplaces of others can play a significant part in fulfilling this need. A leader should watch for anyone becoming isolated, being left out by the other team members, not socialising or talking to others. This person could be in danger of feeling that they did not belong and therefore their motivation would be driven by this need. The employer might find, if they could see the full life picture of such a person, that they fulfil their need to belong in some way outside the workplace and it is this other destination that enjoys the fruits of this individuals motivation (perhaps a voluntary organisation?)

However within the workplace it is common for all three of these fundamental needs to be satisfied and therefore they are no longer motivators. Which begs the question: what does motivate most people in the workplace?

The answer is the two remaining needs, which are *to be respected* and *to be fulfilled*. The great thing about these needs is that they are insatiable, need constantly replenishing and are easy to address. Examples of *how respect and fulfilment are achieved* are:

- Helping people to *achieve* things by solving problems, having recommendations accepted, having meaningful responsibilities and completing difficult tasks.
- Giving people the experience of *being recognised* by receiving praise for specific achievements, gaining respect from others, getting helpful feedback on performance or

being listened to by someone in a more senior role.

- *Participating* by planning and scheduling their own work, establishing their own goals and being part of the organisations decision making.
- Through *personal growth*, being able to increase skills and applying new learning to tasks, and as a result getting new more complex tasks.

All of which fits so neatly with delegation that it should then become obvious that *the leader who delegates (using the correct methods) will always succeed in raising motivation* because that leader is putting people in a position where they will generate motivation for themselves. In contrast, the leader who fails to delegate will be responsible for a decline in motivation.

Both issues of delegation and motivation are inextricably linked and were jointly responsible for the lacklustre meeting in which Eric had found himself.

The meeting had fallen into awkward silence and Glo sat with her head in her hands. Perhaps, she thought, she was living in the dullest place on earth, perhaps nothing happened here.

'For goodness sake,' the words burst from her, 'what's wrong with you people? You just have to do your damn jobs. I can't believe there are no stories.'

'A couple of boys managed to get covered in purple dye at the school.' Eric was speaking. 'I think we got some good pictures.'

Glos shook her head, despairingly.

The group exchanged glances and the silence deepened.

It was Freda who broke it with, 'Did I mention my neighbour's shed?'

Glo groaned and buried her head in her hands. Furtive glances were exchanged around the table before Glo burst into life again, leaping to her feet.

'Right, who's got a shed?'

The question took everyone by surprise.

'Dan? Got a shed in your garden?'

'No Glo.'

'Eric? Joe? Sue? Come on, anyone got a shed?' She paused and when she got no response her volume got louder and tone harsher 'Oh do wake up, someone make an effort.'

The group were shocked, they had never heard Glo in anger before.

Sue ventured 'My grandma's got one, used to be my grandad's before he died. But there's nothing in it now she never uses it, it's on the allotment.'

'Ok, I've got one but it's no good for anything,' said Joe, 'I got a build-it-yourself kit years ago but DIY is not my thing. You can't use it for anything, Glo, the floor slopes and the door doesn't fit properly.'

'Perfect' said Glo.

A telephone rang on a smart desk inside a smart office in a smart city. It was the office of the Managing Director of TAMedia International. Tony Gull knew that the caller must be one of a small group of family or selected business colleagues since this was his direct line, not the switchboard line. A cultured voice greeted him and he felt genuine warmth at the sound of Tom Arnold's voice. The Chairman was pretty much a recluse. Tony hadn't seen him for years but very occasionally received a call from him. Tony liked Tom a lot. They had been journalists together before Tom had lost his wife and son in the accident. Tony saw Tom drive his grief into the energy that built the business, taking Tony with him as a trusted assistant. When Tom decided to step down he was a wealthy man, but it was as if the energy had been all used up, as if he had expunged the pain of his loss and now he could live a different life. Tom chose to keep his new life a secret and, handing over the reigns to Tony, he disappeared. His seven figure salary was still paid to his bank and the only other correspondence or contact that he permitted was to have a set of annual accounts sent to his address in Hong Kong. Tony had no idea where Tom was or how he lived his life.

Tom's faith in Tony had been justified. TAMedia had grown and prospered, acquiring newspapers across a dozen countries and building an attractive and profitable portfolio.

'How are you Tom? Lovely to hear from you.'

'I'm fine, Tony, just fine.'

'Are you keeping well?'

'Busy becoming an old man dear boy.'

The exchange of pleasantries lasted until Tom brought the conversation around to its purpose.

'I believe you have some challenges with the *Town Crier*?'

Tom never ceased to amaze, thought Tony. How on earth did he know about this tiny wrinkle in the TAMedia empire? A small regional paper tucked away in an unlikely corner of just one of the twelve nations in which TAMedia operated.

'I believe we do Tom. You are well informed. I think the National MD for that territory has been scratching his head about that one for some time.'

'I'm sure he has,' said Tom, who had the latest issue of the *Town Crier* laid out before him with its sensational headline SERIAL SHED MANIAC STRIKES DOUBLE BLOW emblazoned across the front cover 'let me suggest a strategy to you...'

Joe was sitting opposite Eric. He had just delivered genuine congratulations to him on getting the Editor's job and an assurance of support.

'Thanks Joe,' replied Eric, 'now I have something to ask of you. I'm going to head office to sort out some things. While I'm away I would like you to run the editorial meetings.'

Joe sat upright in his chair. He had not expected this.

'I've never run one of those meetings before, Eric.'

'I know you haven't and that seems ridiculous to me. After all, you have years of experience in putting together sports pages and back page headlines, why shouldn't you be able to edit the rest of the paper?'

Eric saw that Joe's face was slightly flushed.

'But that's your job now Eric, don't you want to keep that for yourself? After all, you've worked hard enough to get to that position.'

'No Joe, I think it's a job that a few of us need to have experience of. We can talk it through before I go and you can call me while I'm away if you want to discuss anything. I'm confident that you are more than able to do it, and I also think you will learn something by doing this that will help you with your own job.'

'Thanks' said Joe 'I appreciate your trust.'

Eric saw a spark in Joe's eye that had been absent for a long time. He felt Joe was flushed because he was excited.

'It would also be nice to get some of the others up to the standard where they could run the meeting as well – do you think that we could achieve that between us?'

'Of course we could,' said Joe 'It might take a bit of time, but I see what you mean. If we all got to experience the role we might be able to work together better.'

'Yes, they would be more able to contribute.'

Joe didn't expect to get excited at work any more, but within a few short minutes he had become so. He left Eric's office with an urgency in his step that attracted a few surprised looks from those he passed. Just then Eric's phone rang. It was Glo.

'Hi Eric, just rang to wish you well, you deserve it.'

'Thanks Glo, when do you start your new job?'

'Three weeks,' said Glo. 'They are insisting I take two weeks holiday and then I have to attend a management refresher course called 'Delegate to Motivate'. It's all a bit of a surprise but I'm looking forward to my new newspaper.'

Eric replaced the receiver and leaned back in his chair. He was looking forward to making a real difference at the *Town Crier*. He knew how quickly attitudes could change when the real motivators are addressed. He was not surprised at Joe's positive response and was convinced that there were many others whose skills and energy were presently hidden. They had not been motivated because their needs 'to be respected' and 'to be fulfilled' had not been addressed. By means of effective delegation this would change.

In the weeks and months that followed it was not only Joe that got a new spring in his step. So did the *Town Crier* and many more of its employees.

Learning Questions

1. Why didn't working long hours prove a successful strategy for Glo?

2. What is the significance of the Nostalgia team to this story?

3. What did the machine signify that was in the hands of the statue of David Mars?

4. When JB advised Eric that he would feel discomfort when he delegated, what was he talking about?

5. What happened to revive Joe's motivation?

Learning Summary – Delegation

- Delegation can be a powerful source of motivation
- Lack of delegation can be a powerful source of de motivation
- A leader should use delegation to develop and motivate team members
- A good delegation requires the delegator to follow a process that includes
    o Communicating a clear vision of the task
    o Selling the task so that the other person wants it
    o Explaining how and why
    o Setting a realistic timetable
    o Reviewing the delegation and giving constructive feedback
- A good delegation may require the delegator to use assertive communication and coaching

7

Pieces in the Puzzle
(Building a Team)

Part 1

Some instinct caused Henrik to raise his eyes from the newspaper headline and gaze across the busy station foyer. A stranger in the crowd caught his attention. In fact, it wasn't the stranger that caught his attention but the briefcase that the stranger was carrying: it was identical to his own. To reassure himself, he moved his foot to make contact with the case that should have been resting by his seat, and found nothing; it was gone. He leapt to his feet, throwing the newspaper aside in a flutter of pages.

Perhaps it was a similar instinct that prompted the stranger to look back over his own shoulder at precisely this moment. Both men began to run, one in pursuit of the other. The stranger sprinted toward an entrance, knocking people aside and leaving a wake of reeling travellers behind him. He didn't care; he was focussed only on making his escape. Henrik was running as fast he could, but was losing ground to the stranger, who would soon be out of the station and lost amongst the much larger crowds that would be outside.

The outstretched leg that turned events in Henrik's favour was encased in an unforgettable lime green nylon, and finished off with a desert boot. The running stranger was more concerned with finding the nearest exit and checking the progress of the pursuing Henrik to notice the unexpected hurdle. As his own leg made contact with the outstretched limb it was halted in its forward movement, unlike the rest of his body that continued on its journey with considerable momentum. Since you are observing this incident in slow motion you might now imagine the trajectory taken by the stranger's flying body (since both feet had left the ground, pulled forward by the continued motion of his torso). See his arms stretching out to protect himself from the ground that was rushing toward him, the briefcase now released and spinning like a misshapen and badly weighted discus at an angle of forty five degrees to his line of travel. Then the inevitable collision of the flying body with first the ground and then, after a grazing slide across grimy concrete, the ankles of a pair of pensioners who, on being bowled over like nine pins, leapt nimbly to their feet addressing their assailant vigorously with folded umbrellas. Meanwhile the briefcase hit the ground skimming for some distance, to halt at the feet of a startled ticket collector.

In these few seconds Henrik made up the ground and choosing first to retrieve his case, turned to see once again the back of the stranger disappearing into the crowd. This time he did not follow deciding that, with a heavy brief case, he had little chance of catching his man.

'G'day Henrik. Got yourself into some bother already?'

It was the owner of the lime green leg. Henrik instantly recognised Shaz, they had met before at initial interview stage. Once met, Shaz was not someone you would forget, and in this instance he was very pleased to see her.

'So you got Australia, well done. Thanks for your help just now Shaz, I reckon I'd have lost this if you hadn't stopped him.'

'No sweat, I guess you got Sweden?'

'Yes, so are you here also for induction?'

'I am, just not causing as much fuss as you!'

Thankfully for Henrik and Shaz their remaining journey was less eventful and so it was that, having checked into their hotel, they were delivered by chauffeur driven car to the impressive new headquarters of The Game League. The two had previously met when both had attended selection meetings at which hopefuls from various countries were bidding to acquire a Game League franchise. The presentations made by each had been the result of months of work by teams of specialists putting together a high quality business plan to The Game League's demanding standards. Basic requirements were a minimum number of GL stadiums to be completed before the league could be launched; government and community involvement were also specified and each franchise must agree to run and finance their businesses in a particular way and to a specified formula. An unusual facet of the Games League franchise was the insistence that each franchisee committed to manage its employees along agreed guidelines, and today Shaz and Henrik were there to begin a full week's briefing on the subject.

From the aerial photograph displayed in the reception area, Henrik could see that the building's outline was an oval. Its outer walls were built to mirror the shape of the GL stadiums that were springing up around the world, each to exactly the same design and specification. The walls were made from an opaque blue glass and rose magnificently, curving outward as they climbed and then inward again toward the roofline. The roof flattened toward a central point before climbing once again, this time swelling as if pulled upward when molten by a great invisible hand to form an impressive dome that towered high above the entire structure. The dome could be seen as a proud and shimmering statement of success from many miles around. On the outside of the building there were no signs or flags, simply the emblem of The Game League (the outline of a game ball containing within it a pattern of five interlocking cogs, one in the centre and the other four arranged around the outside) etched onto the entry doors.

This calm exterior enclosed a place that was filled with activity. As Henrik and Shaz stepped across the threshold, the fizz of excitement that greeted them was exhilarating. The reception area used the full height of the structure; it had clear glass in the roof that by some means of reflection flooded the space below with natural light. A semi circle of Gamescreens at second story level grabbed the attention of the visitor. Each screen showed images that fed the imagination: exciting moments from game play, stadiums under construction leaping up in high speed sequence, trophies being presented, crowds jumping to their feet to celebrate. To the left of the entrance doors were three receptionists each sitting at a podium and each with two seats opposite them. Shaz and Henrik chose one and the receptionist smiled, inviting them to sit whilst she took their details, prepared an ID pin for each and made their presence known to their host. Once this process was complete they were invited to enjoy the reception area, since they were ten minutes early.

On the opposite side of the reception area was a welcoming refreshment plaza hosting a dozen tables. Some of these were occupied by groups in discussion, perhaps holding meetings, and others by individuals perhaps waiting for a meeting sipping at a drink and enjoying the screens. There were three gaming points that looked like those installed in the stadiums, except that on inspection these had been adapted and were question and answer units. Shaz touched the screen on one, which sent a list of frequently asked questions scrolling before her eyes. She selected a question with a second touch 'How many Game Stadiums are there in the world?' The screen returned: 'Your answer is displayed on Gamescreen four'. She raised her head and there on the fourth screen from the right was her answer: 'THERE ARE 541 GAMES LEAGUE STADIUMS IN THE WORLD TODAY'.

Henrik was still studying the aerial photograph and Shaz was still asking questions when they were interrupted by a friendly and familiar voice. 'Good Morning. Welcome to our new home.'

'Good Morning Jack,' they both replied.

Part 2

Jack's welcoming presence was familiar to Henrik and Shaz from their previous visits. He was a big imposing man with a shock of thick dark hair framing his broad face; this made him look younger than his years. Jack was casually yet fashionably dressed, a dark jacket over a light opened necked shirt. He was one of the team responsible for advising franchisees on new stadium construction.

'This is a pleasure Jack,' Shaz smiled, equally fashionable in her own unique style.

'Glad to see that winning the franchise hasn't changed your dress tastes,' Jack grinned, obviously pleased to see them both.

'I wore my sunglasses especially,' said Henrik.

Today Shaz was in a bright green knitted suit, her hair up Japanese-style with inserted chopsticks and all finished off with the ubiquitous desert boots. Whilst Shaz habitually chose bold colours and unusual combinations, she had the confidence to carry it off. She revelled in the comments that her dress generated; she was a popular and charismatic character. Henrik, in contrast, displayed a quiet Nordic manner that clothed a firm and professional persona. He quickly gained respect and the confidence of others. In his grey suit, white shirt and dark blue tie he was an absolute contrast to Shaz.

'I thought you would be far too busy to be looking after us Jack,' said Henrik.

'Not at all Henrik, all managers take it in turns to host new franchisees – it's something we look forward to. I will be with you for most of the week and it will be my pleasure today to show you around our new building.' He spread his arms to underline his words.

'Yes, last time we were here you were in your old offices,' said Henrik.

'This is The Game League's fourth home since it started 10 years ago. We just keep growing.'

'And have you been here all that time Jack?' asked Shaz

'Well in a manner of speaking yes,' replied Jack. 'I have been with The Game League for a little less than a year but I have worked on this site for most of my life.'

The pair looked puzzled.

'Before this was built there was a factory here, on this very spot. Years ago it was the biggest employer in The Town. I worked for The Factory since leaving school until last year. The building was demolished 12 months ago and the owners sold the land to The Game League. Now The Game League is the biggest employer in The Town and this is the exact spot where the greatest machine in the old factory stood.' They both looked down and saw that they were standing on the cog at the dead centre of a Game League emblem formed as a pattern in the tiled floor. 'The Game League has helped bring The Town back to life in a big way.'

Shaz studied the design beneath their feet. 'How many people work here now?'

'There are almost 1,000 employees on site here, and growing. I'll show you as much as I can over the next few days.'

' I'm looking forward to it,' Henrik replied, gazing up at the images on the Gamescreens, 'and at least your greeting is more friendly than the one I got at the station.'

'Why, what happened?'

'Someone tried to steal my brief case. If Shaz hadn't

helped out I would have lost it. That would have left me in a real mess, it contains a copy of our business plan for Sweden that I need to talk through during my visit.'

'That's odd,' said Jack 'the same thing happened to someone else who was visiting us last week. It's unusual for The Town; we don't get much of that kind of thing.'

Jack turned and indicated a pair of double doors leading out of the reception area. 'Let me take you to meet Judith and Geoff, they are both here to see you today.'

The doors opened automatically as invisible sensors read their ID pins and granted them access. Jack led them into an open plan area, active with busy people and the buzz of conversation. Phones rang, computer screens glowed; there was an infectious optimism in the atmosphere. Shaz and Henrik later learned that the whole building was divided into slices, like a cake prepared for eating, with each slice hosting a different area of responsibility within the organisation – Development, Marketing, Public Relations, International Support, Future Planning. Each slice of the building ran from the outside wall toward the centre, where the circular Development Area was topped by the great dome. The Development Area was for meeting and learning. This flexible area could be transformed into one large and very impressive circular meeting chamber or silently and effortlessly divided by electronically operated mechanisms into separate learning spaces.

Now Jack guided them to meet the two joint Managing Directors of The Game League, the two who had started the whole thing. Geoff and Judith rose to their feet as Jack entered their office with the visitors.

'Good Morning Shaz, Henrik,' said Judith, offering a handshake to both. 'Good morning dad,' she said to Jack.

Part 3

Henrik and Shaz were impressed that both Managing Directors were meeting with them. As Geoff explained the importance of this week, it became clear that they viewed spending time with people as a sound investment.

Judith and Geoff described how they had met at university. Judith had been the sport enthusiast and Geoff the budding business entrepreneur. The two had devised the idea of The Game and got friends to experiment with early versions as they perfected the final winning formula. It was Geoff who had prepared and presented a business case to the financiers of the first stadium; the success of the venture as a one-off was so good that they were soon developing a second and third stadium and along with that the foundations of The Game League. It all sounded so simple but they had taken a big gamble at the time and worked long hours to make it successful.

Judith contributed more than her sporting flair; she brought with her ideas about getting the best from people. She had learned from her father about The Factory and about David Mars, had seen how powerful and successful that had been and how painful the decline was for her father and for The Town. As she grew to adulthood and came to recognise the complexities of human behaviour, these lessons from her youth became more meaningful.

'At first we got it wrong,' said Judith. 'We had to learn that our managers were the key to the organisation. David Mars hadn't left an instruction book on how to do it, we just knew what he had achieved, and wanted that success for ourselves.

We believed that if we could find the Hidden Treasure amongst our own people, it would be the key to that success. The Game League is not this lovely new building, nor is it all those purpose built stadiums: GL is people. But it took us a while to find out how our managers could unlock the real potential within those people.'

'We spoke to some who had worked in The Factory in its glory days,' said Geoff, 'people like Judith's father,' indicating Jack. 'We asked them how things had been run and how people had behaved. We learned that amongst the people that make up any organisation is a critical sub group, the people managers. By this we mean everyone who holds responsibility for the performance of others. At GL that's Judith and I, every manager, supervisor and team leader. We recognised that the most important skills these people need are those that allow them to get the best performance from their people.'

'Once we understood that,' Judith took over the narrative, 'and gave them those skills, our organisation began to spring forward. The change we achieved within a few months was incredible. At first our people changed and then the whole organisation began to change.

Plans for new initiatives were more successful more often. There were fewer mistakes and when mistakes did occur they were corrected quickly and we seemed to learn from them. Skill levels across the organisation rose and there grew a willingness to take responsibility. As a result of all of this we found that our organisation could develop swiftly in new directions, and change was not resisted but welcomed as a source of fresh challenge and success. Quality improved, and it became easier to set and maintain higher standards in every part of what we do.'

'These were the things that set us toward the success that we are enjoying today.' Now Geoff was talking, the enthusiasm demonstrated by the two of them was stimulating. 'The climate, by that I mean the atmosphere between people across our whole organisation, has changed for the better. There are more smiling faces, people share ideas and standards. There is more respect and honesty amongst people, there is frequent and clearly understood communication. These better attitudes spill outside GL; people take them home. We are employing happier, more confident people and our staff turnover is low.'

'What we saw,' said Judith picking up the story again, 'was that people were transformed as a result of the way that they were treated by their managers. Once we recognised that, we put a lot of effort into making sure that everyone holding a managerial role with GL developed the skills needed to help people perform to their true potential. It took us longer to recognise something else, which with hindsight is obvious, that all of our franchisees should also adopt these same ideas and approaches. We asked ourselves what would it be like if the Hidden Treasure within every employee in every GL organisation in the world could be discovered to the advantage of The Game League?'

'It would be amazing,' said Shaz, who to that point had been silently listening to all that had been said by Geoff and Judith.

'That was our conclusion,' said Judith 'so we set about trying to make that happen. At the beginning of this year we introduced the programme that you have come to experience this week. We want you to return to your businesses as ambassadors for this way of working with people, we want to help you so that you can help others to learn these skills.'

'And that,' said Geoff, 'is when we came up with the new emblem. We borrowed the idea of the five cogs from David Mars. One in the centre and the other four arranged around the outside. It represents a human mechanism. It was David Mars's way of showing how people work together. The central cog represents the leader and the whole mechanism shows the influence that leader has on the team, and the influence they have on each other. We liked that, and felt that if David were around today we would have his blessing to use it. By putting that human mechanism at the centre of a Game Ball we wanted to signify that GL is about people and its success depends upon how people behave toward each other. Our subtle addition was the five teeth on the centre cog and this week you will see that the significance of those teeth is about *creating teams*. Your key to finding the hidden treasure is to get your *people helping each other to achieve shared objectives. That is how we define working as a team. Only within a true team can individuals achieve their full potential.* We will show you that there are five pieces that must be placed together like a puzzle and when that is done then people will behave as a team. Each of those five teeth on the central cog represents one of those pieces and this week you will learn about each of them.'

Shaz and Henrik were impressed by Geoff and Judith's explanation. 'I can't wait to get started,' said Shaz.

'You've both had a long day,' Judith stood, pushing her chair aside. 'Tomorrow you will begin, but for tonight I think you need some rest.'

With the meeting closed the pair were escorted by Jack back out to reception. 'I'll see you tomorrow,' he said. 'You have an interesting week ahead.'

This turned out to be an understatement.

Part 4

The GL reception area was alive with laughter and movement when Shaz and Henrik arrived on the following morning. A party of schoolchildren were waiting to begin a guided tour of the new building; they were excited and the volume of sound that they generated reflected this. Many were looking up at the Gamescreens, their chatter and movement increasing on recognition of familiar images or the appearance of a star player. Of the two adults who accompanied them, one seemed as lively as the children, a tall attractive female teacher, with fair shoulder length hair and an open countenance.

Shaz loved a bright atmosphere and led Henrik through the throng to register their arrival with one of the receptionists. Her sky blue trouser suit and desert boots gained some attention (of the nudging and winking variety) from some of the schoolchildren, although Henrik in his grey suit, white shirt and light blue tie passed almost unnoticed.

The school party were soon led into the building. Jack appeared and, greeting Henrik and Shaz, took them to the Development Area. Today the large space had been replaced with smaller rooms into one of which Jack escorted them. When they were comfortably seated, it was Jack who took the lead.

'Your first day will be hosted by me and by some of the other managers who work here. We are going to help you learn about the first of the five teeth on the central cog, the first of the five things that you must do if you are to be successful in getting people to work together as a team. This first thing is *Communication.* We will help you understand how to make *clear communication* between people and most of all how to make *assertive communication* a habit throughout your organisations.'

The day that followed for Henrik and Shaz took them on a journey of understanding around a subject that both thought they already knew. Henrik's natural scepticism had surfaced at the beginning of the day when Jack had announced the subject. But in the following hours they both came to understand how powerful the subject was, and how much they still had to learn. They met various managers from within GL, some of whom took them to their own departments and discussed communication issues with their staff, whilst some told them of their own conversions from passive or aggressive to assertive communicators. They learned that *Assertive Communication is the bedrock of successful team building. Without the ability to communicate assertively, a manager cannot successfully coach or delegate, cannot disagree or make requests, cannot feedback views effectively, cannot give or receive criticism, cannot say 'no', cannot handle aggressive or passive behaviour from others. In short, they cannot lead.* A Passive communicator will avoid most of these things and an aggressive communicator will do them but in doing so will create enemies and non co-operation. A manager cannot put into place the other four elements of team building without being an assertive communicator. And further, a manager must lead all team members to be assertive communicators with each other and with the manager.

The morning flew by and during the afternoon Shaz and Henrik met many people around the GL building who had talked with enthusiasm about the subject.

To finish their day, Jack had asked if they would join with the school group to view a film about the growth and future plans for The Game League. On their return to the

Development Area they found that it had been reconfigured to make an auditorium for the showing of the film. The school group were still energised. They had toured the new building and visited the local Game Stadium and training grounds during the day, meeting some of the players in the process. They had, in short, had a thoroughly exciting day. As they filed into the auditorium, one of the kids said to the lively teacher: 'bet you can't score with that one, Miss Thompson.' The boy was pointing to a Gameball presented in a colourful frame. It was one of a dozen that adorned the walls, each about 2 metres above floor level. Without a further word the teacher rose on her toes extending an open hand and touched the ball with her fingertips. A seemingly innocuous action but then, to the great entertainment of the children and the obvious horror of the teacher, the frame dislodged from the wall and swung downward with just one fixing point remaining intact. Now it heaved dangerously to and fro, threatening to completely break free and clatter to the floor at any moment. What caused the greatest interest was what was revealed in a space behind where the frame had been fixed: there appeared to be a camera and a small pack of other electrical equipment.

It was Jack who broke the hush that had followed. 'Good grief what on earth is that?'

'That looks like some sort of surveillance equipment to me,' said Henrik quietly.

And so it was that, when all visitors had gone and the find had been carefully inspected, it was found to be a surveillance camera and microphone. A small hole had been drilled for the camera to view through. Whoever had planted these devices had failed to properly re-secure the frame and hence its collapse on being touched by the embarrassed Miss Thompson. A professional search of the building found four other such devices. Someone appeared to be taking an unhealthy interest in The Game League.

Part 5

Jack had resisted all questions about the rest of their week.

'You've already got enough to think about,' he had said at the end of their first day. 'Take it a day at a time and let the picture reveal itself.'

So when Shaz and Henrik arrived at the GL Building for their second day they had no idea what lay before them.

Once again they were shown into the meeting room in the Development Area, which this morning was equipped with a television screen. Here Jack introduced them to Mike, a younger fair-haired man who was to be their host for the day. Mike informed them that today they would learn about the second of the five teeth on the central cog, the second of the five things that they must do if they were to be successful in getting people to work together as a team. Mike told them that this was *Leadership*, and that they would begin by watching a television programme on the subject.

Despite his experience of the previous day, Henrik once again felt that this would be a waste of his time. He had a recognised management qualification from a respected university. He knew every theory there was to know about leadership.

Mike switched on a video player and dimmed the lights.

The Game! The Game! THE GAME! – lively music bounced around the bright pictures that delivered the advertising message.

The advertisement finished and was replaced with the announcer's voice – 'In this final episode of the series Unlikely

Leaders, investigative journalist Steve Prince meets perhaps the unlikeliest leader of the series and... loses his moustache.'

For the next thirty minutes Henrik and Shaz were enthralled with the programme that followed. They smiled with Mike at his appearance in the programme as the organiser of a community playground project, and were intrigued with the ideas that were being explained.

'You've come a long way since then,' said Shaz to Mike when the programme was finished.

'Yes,' replied Mike, 'that was filmed twelve months ago. I got the chance of a job at GL a few weeks later. I had been out of work for a long time but what you saw in that programme gave me the knowledge and the confidence to get back into employment. There are a lot of people at GL who had a similar experience.'

'And do you enjoy your work here?' asked Henrik.

'It is tremendous, a great place to work. Almost as good as working with Helen and that is who we are going to meet next.'

'We are going to see the old lady in the film?' they chorused.

'Yes' replied Mike, 'Geoff and Judith asked her to run these sessions on Leadership after seeing the film. We are going on a tour of The Town with Helen, who will show you a lot of the things that have happened with the regeneration project. At the same time she will talk to you about how she led the project and take you to meet some of the other people who have been involved. I guarantee that by the end of today you will have a clear understanding of exactly how leadership can be achieved for real.'

Mike led them out to the front of the building. On their way through reception they met Judith, who was just arriving. She looked worried; it was the first time that Shaz had seen her like this.

'Problem?' asked Shaz.

Judith brightened when she saw Shaz, perhaps it was the way her purple and lilac sari complemented her desert boots or perhaps it was just Shaz's smiling face. 'Not really, let's just call it a challenge!' replied Judith.

Shaz and Henrik were led to a waiting people carrier. The door slid open to reveal an elderly lady seated at a small table within the vehicle.

'Hello dear,' she smiled at Henrik's voice, unable to see his smart grey suit, white shirt and mid blue tie, 'and you dear,' she added as even her feeble eyes registered the splash of bright colour that could only be Shaz behind him, 'climb in and we'll go for a ride.'

As Henrik and Shaz began their day with Helen, drama was unfolding at the GL building.

Geoff has received a late night call from a friendly journalist, 'Read tomorrow's papers. There's a story breaking about corrupt refereeing in The Game League, and rumours that your gaming licence might be threatened.' Geoff was stunned and immediately rang Judith.

By the time they met in the morning, the story had broken and the GL share price was plummeting fast. 'There is no truth in this,' said Judith, 'but someone is out to cause big trouble for us while we prove otherwise.'

Geoff had asked for all calls to be held whilst he and Judith considered the situation. He was therefore surprised when his phone rang 'I'm sorry Geoff, but it's Ian at The Mechanics – he says it's really important and it's not about the press story.'

'Ok put him through.'

'Good morning, Geoff. I'm sure you have enough on your plate today but you need to see what's just arrived in my mail.'

'Your phone bill?' Geoff had always been able to maintain

his sense of humour under pressure but he was about to be tried to the extreme.

'No Geoff. It's an offer to defect to a new league and the terms are fantastic – I'll fax it through.'

Moments later a copy of the documents that Ian had received lay on the desk before the two managing directors. They were aghast at what they read. The offer was to join a new league with a financial package that almost doubled income for the clubs' owners. In addition, the plan for the new league had a whole range of great ideas that the document claimed would enhance The Game and build greater profitability; Geoff and Judith were shocked because they recognised these as The Game League's own ideas, developed painstakingly by employee improvement teams over many months and about to be published to all franchisees next week. It seemed those responsible for the surveillance equipment were making themselves known.

The offer was from BleakCorp who, having teamed up with one of the worlds largest sports clothing manufacturers, made a formidable enemy and a credible sponsor for an alternative game league.

For Shaz and Henrik the day was also proving challenging, but in a positive way. Helen explained to them how effective Leadership was an essential element for successful team building. It is *the role of the leader to ensure that each of the five elements is in place.* This does not mean that the leader has to do all of these things, just make sure that they are done. This is why the leader must understand the five elements. She showed them the fundamentals of Leadership, explaining the real meaning and implications of fulfilling *task, team and individual needs,* alongside displaying appropriate *traits of personality.*

They began to see how the five elements depended upon each other. Without the ability to communicate assertively, a manager could not show effective leadership. To demonstrate good leadership, a leader must insist upon and obtain assertive communication throughout a team.

At the end of their day with Helen, they were charmed and impressed by this elderly lady who knew so much and had the achievements to prove it. They returned to their hotel to consider what they had seen and heard, and to wonder what lay ahead.

Back at the GL building Geoff and Judith were having a less satisfying experience. By lunchtime the trickle of calls from club chairmen had become a torrent, all having read the press and all having received the offer from BleakCorp. Amongst these calls came one that was particularly unwelcome.

'It's the chairman of BleakCorp,' announced Geoff's assistant.

On completing a succinct conversation, Geoff put down the phone. He looked toward Judith, his face flushed.

'It looks like we're being hijacked. BleakCorp are going to make a bid for us. It seems they've secretly been buying up shares under other names for weeks. He says that if we sell they will offer us yesterday's share value and call off the new league. If we don't, more of these stories will be 'leaked' to the press and they'll put a forty eight hour deadline on club chairmen to accept the offer to join the new league. He's threatening to tear the Game League apart.'

Part 6

Jack was driving the sleek silver car that collected Henrik and Shaz from their hotel; he was taking them to the Mechanics Game Stadium.

'*Skills and Knowledge* today,' said Jack. 'That's the third tooth on the cog, the third of the five things that you must achieve if you are to be successful in getting people to work together as a team.'

'It feels like we're getting somewhere now Jack – Communication, Leadership and now Skills and Knowledge.' Shaz was gazing out of the window as the car passed the neat houses and trim gardens of a residential street and thought that the Town was already beginning to feel familiar.

'You'll soon be experts,' smiled Jack and then continued. 'We have a special situation today, a Whole Organisation Message and as visiting members of the GL family it's for me to include you in the process.'

'Sounds mysterious, Jack,' replied Henrik. 'What is a Whole Organisation Message?'

'It's what happens when we have information that needs to go to everyone. There are just four communications, four discussions, between Judith and Geoff and every employee, including those at all the franchised clubs. It's a good test of the quality of our team working to get a message to travel accurately through the organisation. We have a method of ensuring that important information travels from Geoff and Judith, through managers and team leaders, to every employee arriving just as it started with no misunderstandings and at great speed. And you are now included in that process.'

Jack proceeded to tell them what had happened yesterday – the lack of truth in the newspaper story, the dropping share price, the offer to defect to a new league, the ideas stolen from GL, the involvement of BleakCorp and the sports wear manufacturer, BleakCorp's unwelcome offer, their threat to 'leak' more stories and to put pressure on the club chairmen.

Henrik was shocked at what he heard and surprised that Judith and Geoff were prepared to tell every employee in the business all of this. When he questioned Jack on this, the reply made Shaz smile, she was beginning to understand the true significance of the cogs. Jack's reply was 'How can we all help if we don't know the problem?'

But Henrik still didn't get it 'What do you mean help? This is in the hands of the directors now. They are the ones who must sort this out. We just have to hope they get it right.'

Now it was Jack's turn to smile. 'I see we haven't yet got our message across to you, Henrik. I had better deliver you to Ian and Alice for your next lesson.' So saying they drove into the car park of The Mechanics Game Stadium and Jack was soon introducing Shaz and Henrik to the club's managing director and team coach. They were used to colour and style at the stadium but nevertheless the arrival of Shaz clad in orange mini skirt, bright blue blouse and matching tights made one or two of the young apprentices sit up and take notice; the desert boots always came as a shock. Henrik however in his grey suit, white shirt and deep blue tie made a more understated arrival.

It was a busy morning at the GL building. The place was buzzing as the Whole Organisation Message flushed the important news of yesterday's developments through the people who were The Game League and its franchisees.

Geoff and Judith had not for one moment considered capitulating to BleakCorp, instead they would put their faith in the power of those people. They would do everything possible to release the creative energy of their organisation and fight back against their attackers.

By midday things had changed. There was an excitement in the air. Under threat, every team within GL had directed its attention toward the challenge of resisting BleakCorp. Every employee worked in several teams: their local work teams, other local work teams that they played a role in and then the overall GL team to which they all belonged. Each one of those teams was a true team, not simply a title hanging hopefully over a disparate group of people, but a group of people helping each other toward common goals. Aided by swift and accurate communication, these teams moved quickly and worked together as one formidable force. Any ghost that might have lingered on the site of the GL building from times past would have recognised the spirit of The Mechanism, the great powerful machine rising again, but this time the new mechanism was made of people. This new mechanism was bringing a power to GL that would take its enemies unaware. While other organisations might struggle like great hulking monoliths to slowly alter direction, GL despite its great size could sprint, stop and turn, and in so doing direct its awesome gaze and power on its enemy whilst that enemy was still considering its next move. The speed of reaction of this new mechanism was stunning, and The Game League was fighting back before the dinosaur that was BleakCorp had time to draw breath.

It was the ideas. Problem solving through idea generation was a tried and tested concept within GL. Idea generation was driven by an Improvement Team, a non-managerial team whose representatives gathered ideas from team members and brought them together as recommendations to management. In this way GL was constantly developing every corner of the organisation and the service that it provided. Now the Improvement Teams were focussed on BleakCorp and by early afternoon the ideas were flowing toward Judith and Geoff.

Henrik and Shaz had enjoyed their time with Ian and his team coach Alice. Their story of how they had discovered that the coaching techniques used by Alice with her players could be transferred for use with all club employees was intriguing. Ian explained to them that *coaching was of importance because of the need to maintain the Skills and Knowledge of all team members so that they could properly fulfil their role in the team.*

Ian posed an important question: 'What would happen if the skills or knowledge of one your team members was not good enough to allow them to do their job correctly?'

Shaz answered 'They would let the rest of us down – we wouldn't be able to rely on them?'

'Yes,' said Ian, 'and then what would happen?'

'I suppose it would cause conflict, people would resent them or begin to dislike them.'

'And what would happen to the team?'

'It would start to break down, people would leave the poor performer out of the team,' now it was Henrik answering.

'How do you think the team members would view the leader?'

'I think they would lose respect for the leader. After all, you would expect the leader to sort it out, either get that person's skills up to speed or, if they didn't have the basic ability, get someone else into the team who had or could develop the skills that were needed.'

'And what about a leader who allows team members to

carry on with insufficient knowledge, for example about the product or the market?' Ian's persistent questions were leading Henrik to find the answers for himself.

'Well, that person is not a good leader. They are not fulfilling Team Needs, we learned that yesterday with Helen.'

'What should a leader do to make sure that all team members have the right level of skills and knowledge?'

'Be regularly reviewing their performance and giving them coaching or arranging coaching for them in areas of weakness.'

'That's right, and people don't just need coaching to learn new skills, they need coaching to keep their skills sharp. Just like an athlete who must keep practising even after winning a gold medal.'

'Ok, I think I understand this now,' said Henrik. '*Each team member needs the skills and knowledge to be able to do their job. The leader must use coaching to achieve and maintain consistently high levels of skills and knowledge* and that is why coaching is such an important subject. This is the third tooth on the central cog, the third element that the leader must put in place to build a team.'

'I couldn't have put it better myself,' replied Ian. 'I must also tell you that I only learned all this about a year ago. I had got to a point where I was really struggling to get team working within the club, and as a result the performance of our organisation off the pitch was poor and getting worse. Alice helped me to understand the importance of coaching and then I found that The Game League used this idea as part of a bigger picture for team building. That's when I suggested to Geoff and Judith that they should share this thinking with all club chairmen. They agreed and introduced the programme that you are experiencing this week.'

'So we've got you to thank for all this hard work,' said

Shaz her smile betraying the insincerity of her complaint.

Judith and Geoff had spent the afternoon in conference, considering the many ideas that were being presented to them from around the GL organisation. Throughout the afternoon they had received messages of loyalty from club chairmen. The content of most was that it didn't matter how much BleakCorp offered they would not be interested in turning their backs on the winning formula and the great environment that was The Game League.

By the end of the day many actions were being taken around the organisation to counter the BleakCorp threat. These actions were all ideas generated by the Improvement Teams, approved by Geoff and Judith, and swiftly put into action. The speed of thought and deed would be astonishing to an outsider: press releases were going out in every region; packs had been prepared and sent to every club reminding them of the impressive track record for development of profitable new ideas that GL had achieved over the last couple of years; telephone calls were being made to suppliers, players, and club employees at all levels, and much more as idea after idea arrived with the joint managing directors, and those approved were returned to be implemented.

As a result, the whole place was greatly invigorated when Shaz and Henrik arrived back at the GL building. They were immediately excited by what they saw and by the emotions they sensed. Judith had left word at reception that they were invited to join them, so Jack escorted the pair to the office in which Judith and Geoff were working. They were warmly greeted and Geoff explained what was going on showing them the lists of ideas that were still arriving.

'If you want to see the power of team work, then take a look around this building today,' he said to them.

'What about this one?' interrupted Judith, who was

ploughing through her umpteenth list of ideas that afternoon, 'fight fire with fire.'

'What's the idea?' asked Geoff

'Perhaps the idea is to get some rubbish in the press about BleakCorp just like they did about us,' chipped in Shaz .

'We won't stoop to their level,' Judith looked up from the lists.

'No,' said Geoff, 'but what if there was some genuine stuff about BleakCorp? I seem to remember a whisper of something about a year ago.'

'And?' Judith had stopped reading and was looking at Geoff.

'I should have thought of this earlier. I'll talk to Eric Harley at the *Town Crier* perhaps he can help us.'

'Isn't good old Glo the editor there any more?' asked Judith.

'No Jude, she got moved a year ago. Hey there's another idea, didn't she get moved to the town where BleakCorp are based?'

Part 7

A relentless rain slithered down the hotel window. It was a lazy wetness that lacked the energy or initiative to make an honest splat, but instead drifted aimlessly under a low grey sky, smearing whatever it touched with a half-hearted dampness.

'Perhaps I'm tired after this weeks excitement but I just don't feel motivated today,' said Shaz, resting her chin on her palm and gazing at some invisible point in the distance. Even the vivid orange pinstripes in her navy blue business suit failed to enliven her mood.

The waiter, by now familiar with the pair, raised no eyebrow at Shaz's desert boots this morning, and noted that Henrik was once again smartly attired in his predictable grey suit, white shirt and blue striped tie. Henrik also found himself feeling unusually flat this morning, confronted by Shaz's low mood and the cheerless weather.

It was then that a ray of sunshine burst into the breakfast room. 'Good morning both,' Jack beamed at them and reached out a hand to shake each of theirs in greeting. 'Time to get going, you've got a busy day ahead.'

Henrik felt his mood lift in the presence of Jack's buoyant attitude, and he noted that Shaz also raised a smile in response and began to look a little more like her usual cheerful self.

On arrival at the GL building, it was as if the clouds had completely dispersed. The atmosphere around the building was infectiously positive, and Henrik observed to himself how easy it is for your mood to be changed by the mood of others.

He had been effected negatively by Shaz over breakfast and then again positively by Jack.

'Great feeling here today, Jack,' said Henrik, as they made their way to Geoff's office.

'Yes,' replied Jack, 'we refer to it as 'the climate', by that we mean the atmosphere amongst the team members. A good climate is a natural outcome of good teamwork; a poor climate is a certain sign that people are not working as a team. The leader has a big impact on climate.'

'How is that?' asked a curious Shaz.

'It's a matter of communication, and what we do is probably more important in this respect than what we say. For example, if a leader arrives at work in the morning looking glum, this will inevitably affect the attitude of the team members. The leader may not realise what he or she is doing, they may just be deep in thought, but the facial expression and body language is interpreted by the team as negative. If a leader does not lead a positive climate by actions and attitude, it is likely that the team will begin to reflect whatever attitude the leader is demonstrating.'

Both Shaz and Henrik put a smile on their faces as they entered Geoff's office and received a smile in return. The meeting got off to a good start.

Geoff told them that today's subject would be *common working practices*, and that this was the fourth tooth on the cog, 'the fourth of the five things that you must achieve if you are to be successful in getting people to work together as a team.' He read the looks on their faces. 'You were expecting something a little more exciting?'

'Well, it does sound a bit dull,' said Shaz. Henrik nodded his agreement.

'Lets call it simple rather than dull,' said Geoff.

'OK Geoff, so what's so special about common working

practices?' asked Henrik.

'Do you have common working practices in your organisation Henrik?'

'Yes, of course. You mean things like what time we start work and how we answer the phone?'

'That's just what I mean. Everything that you expect people to do in the same way.'

'That could be a long list,' said Shaz. 'Things like how we communicate with each other, how we complete reports or documents, health and safety procedures.'

'You will find that it is a long list Shaz. My next question for you both is who has decided those working practices?'

The two paused to consider their answers. 'The managers and the directors,' said Henrik. 'Both might have decided these things. But these working practices may have developed over a long time.'

'Yes, that is often true, but for a group of people to work as a team, each member of that group must understand those working practices and agree to follow them. What do you think will happen when members of a group don't understand or don't agree?'

Shaz replied: 'I guess they don't follow them.'

'Yes,' said Geoff, 'and what effect might that have on the other group members?'

'They wouldn't like it, it would be annoying, it would cause them problems – if you all agree to record certain details on a form and one person doesn't do it, then you can't rely on that person can you?'

'Or if someone keeps arriving late in the morning,' said Henrik, 'everyone else starts to think: 'why should I arrive on time?''

'Good,' Geoff again, 'and how might that effect team working?'

'Team working would break down,' replied Shaz. 'No

question about that. If you can't trust someone to do what they're supposed to do, then you don't really want to work with them, you won't be inclined to help them out when they need it and you would do a lot more by yourself because you couldn't trust them to do it.'

'Sounds like the voice of experience,' said Geoff.

'Yes, I've had to work with people like that. Everyone just gets fed up with them and you're right, team working doesn't stand a chance.'

'So what must be done?' said Henrik

'You need to get every member of the team to understand and agree with your working practices. The best way I know to do that is to involve them in setting those working practices.'

'But what about where you already have those things agreed?'

'Get the team to review them. Say something like: 'I would like us to review the way we work together' and give them some area of work to think about. Tell everyone that you want their views and give them twenty four hour's notice. When it comes to the meeting, the leader chairs the meeting but tries to say as little as possible. The leader has to get discussion going, make sure agreements are reached and add in anything that seems important that the team seems to miss.'

Now Henrik spoke. 'I see. Because this way the team has discussed and decided the working practices, so they all understand them and presumably they all agree with them.'

Shaz was speaking now. 'Yes, I can see that too. It's quite different to being told how things must work, and I bet that when anyone doesn't follow what has been agreed, you don't need the manager to step in and say something because the team says it themselves.'

'That is true,' said Geoff. 'The leader has far less to do in terms of maintaining discipline, because the team does it themselves.'

'I can see why this is one of the five elements now. *It is essential that people working together have common working practices or else they will not work smoothly together and will lose confidence in each other.*'

'That's exactly right. Now I am going to send you round the building to talk to some of the managers and team leaders about this. Just like the other days, if you can see the theory working in practise, this well help you understand better.'

Henrik and Shaz were becoming familiar with the GL building and many of those that worked within it. It seemed that all managers had been briefed about their visit and all were happy to help in explaining the subjects that the two were learning. Since every manager had also been through the same learning process and used the principles on a daily basis, each proved to be an effective coach. It was the practical part of these days that really helped to make sense of the learning, thought Henrik. When things were explained to them they were just theories, when you saw them in practise then understanding followed.

Several managers explained how they had experienced a lack of co-operation from team members on working practices. Most of the problems had involved mundane things: keeping working areas tidy, how telephones were answered, how messages were dealt with – lists of simple day-to-day issues. But Shaz could see that these small things could become big irritants if individuals followed different practices or standards. In all cases, the managers described how they had largely eradicated these problems by getting the team to reset working practices. They also described how this contributed to a significant improvement in team climate.

Another day flew by, and as they moved between departments they became aware of a mounting anticipation about the impending official opening of the new building. Representatives from each nation that had a GL League would be attending with some of their star players. It would be an exciting day for the staff and a great photo opportunity for the press.

When Geoff had finished his meeting with Shaz and Henrik, and was once again alone in his office, he lifted the phone.

'Good Morning, is that the *Town Crier*? ...would you put me through to Eric Harley please'.

Part 8

'Good Morning everyone, thanks for being prompt.'

'Morning Eric,' replied various voices from around the oak panelled meeting room.

'Has everyone got the notes I asked you to bring?'

General nods from around the room.

'I had a call from The Game League yesterday; they're in trouble. GL are the biggest employer in this town and you can bet that if BleakCorp get control that will change. You've all seen the press stories in the last few days, but my instinct says there's a bigger and better story to be found – about BleakCorp. I think we can help, not by dressing up some piece of nonsense, but with a real hard hitting story. That's why I have asked you to find your notes from the last editorial meeting that Glo ran.' Around the room the editorial team were giving Eric their full attention. 'We all know that we weren't working as a team back then.' Nods from around the room. 'Today I believe we are.'

'No doubt about it,' said Sue the Features Editor.

'Good then, lets all think back, lets run that meeting again and lets see if we have a story. Come on Joe you start us off.'

' I can remember without my notes,' said Joe, the Sports Editor. 'That meeting was on the morning after a big match. The Mechanics won playing some stunning new moves. There's nothing in that, but since you mention BleakCorp, they were the corporate sponsors on that night and I did see their Chairman on his way to the hospitality area.'

'Anything unusual about that Joe?'

'He had a very attractive young girl on his arm. It was either his daughter or he was up to no good,' replied Joe with a grin on his face, which began to fade as he looked around at the others some of whom had sat forward with particular interest.

Sue, the Features Editor, was most animated by what Joe had said. 'On that day we were finishing a piece on fashion modelling. I was annoyed at being in the meeting because the deadline was tight and I had an interview to complete with a famous fashion model who was visiting The Town on that day. As it happened, she had attended the match on the previous evening as a guest of the club, but I had no idea she was with the BleakCorp Chairman.'

'You know that a scandal very nearly broke about the Chairman of BleakCorp at that time last year?' said Alun the Business Editor. 'There were rumours about a series of affairs with young women, but no one could get enough information to make it worth going to print – he's got a history of suing the press and a bank balance to fund it. Everyone in the media knew something was going on, but no one dared publish.'

'I had a story on the go about BleakCorp at that time,' said Dan, the News Editor, 'but I kept quiet because I wanted to get it myself without Glo taking over. You know what she was like.'

'What was the story, Dan?' asked Eric.

'Well it just fizzled out, but it was an ex-accountant from BleakCorp who was apparently blowing the whistle on some sort of accounting irregularities. Turned out Glo knew the guy but by the time I found that out she had left.'

'I could have helped with that,' said Alun, sitting forward, 'that's business news, you should have spoken to me about it.'

'I think we got some pictures of him with the girl,' said Joe.

'And you never submitted them!' Sue's tone was sharp.

'Well, he wasn't playing for the team was he? It just didn't seem relevant, after all no one had mentioned this story.' Joe looked round the room defensively.

'Hold on, everyone,' said Eric, 'Let's just calm down. First, take this as one more lesson in the importance of team working. We weren't a team then, so mistakes and missed opportunities were inevitable. Do you think we've got enough between us to deliver today?'

A chorused 'Yes' came from around the room.

'Great, so do I, and I'll call Glo for good measure and see if she can help us with the accountant.'

There was a hum of excitement, people were getting up to leave, talking excitedly and heading off to complete tasks that would nail the story.

Freda the crossword compiler was the only one who wasn't part of the activity.

'I'm sorry, Freda,' said Eric. Everyone paused. 'We got carried away; I didn't ask you what your notes said. Did you have anything to add?'

'To be honest, Eric, it seems from my notes that I was engrossed in finishing the puzzle I was working on. It was puzzle 1040.' She paused as if there was some special significance and then said to the blank faces, that's one a week for 20 years, it was my anniversary puzzle.' The team felt a pang of guilt since none had noticed the passing of this moment for Freda, who had been at *The Crier* longer than any of them. 'I just have the last clue noted down,' she added.

Eric smiled; he liked Freda. He had no idea why he kept her coming to the meetings and she rarely had anything to contribute but she was somehow a part of their culture. 'Go on Freda, read us the clue,' he said.

'Remove the physical education from the landscape to cause a shake up,' she replied.

Eric's brow creased in thought, and he looked around the room for help but found none. 'No, you'll have to give me more on that one, you know crosswords drive me crazy. But if you don't tell me,' he added, 'I will be thinking about the damn thing all day.'

Freda sighed a schoolmistress's sigh and looked over the top of her glasses at the gathered journalists. 'What did you call physical education at school?'

'PE,' said Sue.

'Thank goodness,' said Freda. 'It's an anagram: take PE away from landscape and shake it up, move the letters around. And the answer is the sort of thing that can cause a shake up, a big shake up. Now I can't give you any more clues, short of printing it in bold letters across the headline of our newspaper!'

Henrik and Shaz were enjoying their week. The concept of the treasure hidden within people, a great untapped resource, had seemed fairy tale stuff when it was first described to them by Geoff and Judith. As the week progressed, they were becoming convinced.

Jack had met them at the GL reception and once again reminded them of the significance of the central cog in the GL emblem. He told them that today's subject would be *motivation*, and that this was the fifth and final tooth on the cog, 'the last of the five things that you must achieve if you are to be successful in getting people to work together as a team.'

It was Judith who had met with them today and spent time explaining the principles of motivation and its relevance to team building.

She told them about the five needs and emphasised the particular importance to a manager of fulfilling the needs 'to be respected' and 'to be fulfilled'. They had spent much time discussing exactly how this could be achieved, and then Judith had sent them on a tour of the building to see the principles in practise. They met several managers who each explained exactly how they had achieved motivation using the principles that Judith had described. It was seeing motivated people and understanding what happened in the workplace to make them that way that hammered home the lessons that Judith was helping them understand. Later that afternoon they met Judith again who spoke with them about the relevance of Motivation to Team Building.

'A manager can make sure that each of the other four elements for successful team building are in place but if the team don't want it to happen, then it won't. It is the fifth element that brings the whole thing to life; without it, nothing happens. The team must be motivated to expend energy on making it happen. *It is the ability of a manager to motivate that brings the whole process of team building to life.*

'Human beings are creatures of huge potential but so many do not realise that potential. The potential is multiplied with a group of people, but without motivation nothing will happen.

'Think about a space rocket – a huge investment of time, ideas and money, sitting on the launch pad, silent and lifeless. Only when it is energised can all that potential have a value, only when it is fuelled and ignited can the rocket achieve its great potential. It's the same thing with a team of human beings, and the fuel and ignition are the things that create motivation. That's why it is so important for managers to understand what really motivates and how to motivate. Otherwise our team of people is like a space rocket without energy. Huge potential going to waste.'

As the session was finishing, Henrik said: 'Judith, I must ask you something. I am astonished that you have had the time to spend with us. We know what serious matters you are involved with right now and yet you have spent several hours with us. How is this possible?'

'Delegation, Henrik,' she replied. 'Delegation is one of the best motivational tools you can use, I'm sure you must have seen this today as you met others around the GL building.'

With that answer the ideas that had been shown to him during the day all fell into place. He had seen lots of examples of delegation directly motivating people by placing them in a position where they could gain respect and fulfilment. He could also see that by delegating, managers freed themselves to do the most important things (and often those things were about people management). That was why Judith had found time to be with them: she saw her meeting with them as of priority importance, and delegation had allowed her to create the time to do it.

SCANDAL

'Ayooomybya iandal.'

Shaz jumped at the unexpected yell.

She had been engrossed in thoughts about her day when her eyes had been caught by the banner headline on the newspaper billboard, and then came the yell.

She turned to come face to face with a man after her own heart. She knew this instantly because of the colour scheme that greeted her gaze. The newspaper seller was bedecked in a canary yellow shirt emblazoned with crimson parakeets. His legs on this warm Autumn day were only partly covered in calf length beach shorts of an intense blue. It was the desert boots that held her eye.

'G'day,' she said, offering payment and receiving in return an evening edition of the *Town Crier* with the single word SCANDAL emblazoned across its front cover in bold black type.

'Looks like a big story,' continued Shaz, making conversation.

Tom always replied to those who spoke with him beyond the 'paper please mate' level, since very few did.

'Aussie?' he asked.

'Beach bum?' she replied.

Shaz was delighted to see the craggy face burst into a most remarkably animated smile.

Part 9

It was one of those crisp autumn days that refreshes the spirit. The sun shone, trees and buildings were etched with pinpoint clarity against the brightest of blue skies, and the air had a cold edge that was a delight to inhale.

'I thought we would walk today,' said Jack. 'It's such a beautiful day...' he stopped dead in his tracks when he saw them both. He thought he had come to grips with Shaz's wardrobe, but today she had surpassed herself.

'I needed to liven him up a bit,' said Shaz, while Henrik simply shrugged at Jack and smiled a smile of resignation. Henrik was dressed in his expected grey suit and white shirt, but today he was wearing a rich red tie that gave him a quite different and bold appearance (he had refused the offered desert boots). This however was not the end of the story, since Shaz had made a shopping expedition into The Town's burgeoning shopping area and found herself a suit and shirt to match Henrik's. She had also bought two rich red ties and consequently the pair presented a head turning double act, with Henrik the involuntary straight man.

Jack was collecting Shaz and Henrik from the hotel on their final day, which also happened to coincide with the official opening of the new GL building.

'Come along,' said Jack, recovering his poise, 'it's just a ten minute stroll.'

'That will be good,' agreed Henrik, 'a chance for a last look at The Town before we go.'

The three set off from the hotel, which was itself an interesting building. It had been The Town's original library.

Shaz was intrigued by an old brass plate on the street frontage recording how it had been built with money raised by public subscription. Now the building made a small high quality hotel of a type that put the big groups to shame.

They turned onto the main street and began to walk, passing rows of shops that looked prosperous.

'What news have you got for us today, Jack?' asked Shaz.

'Take a look,' replied Jack stopping outside a newsagent and indicating the national newspapers arrayed with their headlines on display. Every one featured BleakCorp. The tabloids had pictures of a provocatively dressed young woman, one had the same woman on the arm of the Chairman of BleakCorp, some of the broadsheets appeared to be referring to other issues at BleakCorp.

UNIMODEL!

CORP IN THE ACT

CHEATED WIFE STANDS BY CHAIRMAN

SHAREHOLDERS DEMAND INVESTIGATION

'I wouldn't like to be the chairman of BleakCorp this morning,' said Shaz.

The trio walked on, chatting over the dramatic events of the week. The buildings on their right gave way to the open greenery of a park. A statute standing just inside the wrought iron gates caught Henrik's attention. It wasn't the full statue that had captured his interest but the item in the hands of the figure that the statue depicted. 'Hey, there's The Game League emblem. Is this meant to be Geoff?'

'No,' Jack laughed, 'that's not Geoff, it's David Mars. Remember I told you that we used his image of the five cogs?'

Shaz was studying the inscription. 'Helping people to do a better job,' she read. 'That's neat. I'll remember that, it really sums up the role of the leader.'

On they walked, passing a school playground teaming with lively children waiting for school to start. On a glorious morning such as this the laughter and energy that came through the mesh fence was equally as invigorating as the bright sunshine. They stopped for a moment, engaged by this splash of life. A chubby red headed boy with glasses and a tall lanky boy, with that awkward thinness of frame that some adolescents experience before filling out to manhood, were the centre of attention for a group of friends standing by the fence. They looked like physical opposites, but their laughter and joking showed a friendship between them. Jack hoped that these kids could learn David Mars's lessons before they left the safety of school for the wider world. Perhaps The Game League could help with this; he would mention it to Judith and Geoff.

They saw the dome of the GL building rising above surrounding structures and, as they walked along the approach road, the full building came into view. On this particular morning, with the light so clear and the sky so bright, the building looked stunning. The blue outer colouring shimmered; the graceful shapes conjured by its architects announced more than success. The building seemed proud with a quiet strength and confidence.

The reception area was already full of life and a chatter of different languages added to the soundscape. One of the Gamescreens was carrying a 24-hour TV news channel reporting the scandal that had broken at BleakCorp. It seemed that each new revelation was leading to another as the media feasted on the stories that were unfolding before them.

When Geoff arrived at the office that morning, he was met by a grinning Judith.

'Looks like you've got some good news, Jude,' he said.

'I just had a call from the Managing Director of the

sportswear company that were supporting BleakCorp's new league. He rang to apologise, they heard about the underhand tactics that BleakCorp have been using. They want nothing to do with that kind of business practise, and have withdrawn their offer to support an alternative league. They would like to come and talk to us about working more closely together.'

Geoff gave Judith a hug. For the last ten years, building The Game League had been their life and the prospect of losing it had been frightening.

'It looks like we've won,' he said.

'I'm certain we have,' said Judith, 'and from the way the media are attacking BleakCorp today I think they're in big trouble. That first scandal seems to have set stories about them running like toppling dominoes, one leading to another. Now they're talking about financial irregularities, and other problems in some of their subsidiaries.'

Business was getting back to normal at The Game League. Henrik and Shaz took the chance to say their goodbyes to new friends around the building. By late morning they found themselves in the reception area amongst a throng of excited GL employees and visitors. They both recognised the faces of well-known players from numerous countries and were excited to stand with everyone outside the main doors for the great group photograph that would officially record the event and be sent to the clubs and media around the world.

Geoff and Judith were about to cut a symbolic ribbon that was stretched across the doorway. Judith was finishing a speech.

'The last few days have been a valuable reminder of how we must keep team working as a central theme in the running of our organisation. We must work tirelessly to ensure that everyone understands the principles that the five teeth on this central cog represent,' she indicated the GL emblem that was etched large onto the entry doors 'and that we constantly put them into practise. *Communication, Leadership, Skills and Knowledge, Common Working Practices and Motivation;* let me remind you that *only when each is in place will any group of people begin to work as a team.* By team working we mean helping each other toward a common goal. When any of these five is missing, then team working will be undermined and begin to fail. As long as we remember this and keep it at the heart of our culture, then we will benefit from the fabulous potential that lies within us all. We will always be able to see the people who work for GL as an asset rather than a liability. Organisations like BleakCorp should be a lesson to us, they should remind us that when this principle is lost, when people cease to perform in teams, then individuals will start to perform below their ability and the entire organisation will be weakened as a result. Now I am delighted to ask Geoff to join me and for us both to officially open this building.'

With that she and Geoff stood forward to cut the ribbon.

'With particular thanks to our architect and builders,' said Geoff. 'It is exactly one year to the day since the last building on this site was demolished, it has been a tremendous achievement by them to finish this building to schedule.'

They cut the ribbon, eliciting a great cheer from those gathered. To Jack's ear it sounded defiant, a cheer of confidence and ambition.

Shaz and Henrik were standing in the reception area, saying their goodbyes to Judith and Geoff.

'Are you both happy to send your managers to experience the programme that you have enjoyed this week?' asked Judith.

Both agreed that they were.

'I learned from Ian at The Mechanics,' said Shaz, 'that

Henrik and I have to be the head coach when our teams get back from the programme. They will come here and learn what we have learned, and then it is for us to keep that learning going back home.'

'That's just right,' said Geoff, 'and if you fulfil that role using the five elements of team building as your guide you will have great success.'

Henrik and Shaz turned to say their goodbyes to Jack and found him daydreaming. He was standing on the central cog of the GL emblem, legs planted apart, his solid frame motionless, strong arms by his side, his hands relaxed, a smile on his face.

'Goodbye, Jack,' said Shaz, extending her hand. Jack turned to face her and took her hand.

'Goodbye,' replied Jack, smiling at her.

'Goodbye, Jack, and thank you for your help,' said Henrik, extending his own hand.

'It was a pleasure to be able to help you both learn,' said Jack.

Learning Questions

1. What is the significance of the five teeth on the central cog of GL's logo?
2. What were the GL people able to do well under pressure because they worked as a team?
3. Which of the five elements did Geoff explain and why is it important?
4. Four of the elements required to build a team had been discussed in previous chapters. What are they?
5. The Mechanism in Chapter 1 is a metaphor. What did it become in Chapter 7?

Learning Summary – Team Building

- A team is a group of people helping each other toward a common goal
- A team will usually outperform a group
- A leader can build a team by ensuring that five elements are in place. Those elements are:
  o Team Leadership
  o Effective Communication
  o Skills and Knowledge
  o Common Working practices
  o Motivation
- Each element requires understanding and effort by the leader and the other team members
- Understanding these five elements allows a would be leader to understand why a group is not working as a team and correct the situation

8

I Made That Happen

The Story

The purpose of this story has been to make you think about how people behave within organisations, and how that behaviour is affected for good and bad by the way they are managed.

You have seen how Assertive Communication, Effective Leadership, Coaching to build and maintain Skills and Knowledge, Delegation to create Motivation, and Common Working Practices all play a fundamental part in the creation of Teams and Team Working. You have seen how in teams, people can be helped most effectively to perform to their full potential. The story is intended to show possibilities. Some will say that these are flights of fancy, or at least exaggerate what can be achieved. Perhaps some will say that 'in the real world' it doesn't work like this. I disagree.

Whilst the storyline may be fictional (as far as I know The Game has not yet been invented, but it's only a matter of time!), the underlying occurrences are all real, they happen, they have happened throughout the history of mankind and will continue to happen, since they are triggered by human nature. If in doubt, you need only look through the social histories of communities that have thrived and blossomed and then shrunk and festered to find plenty of comparisons for The Town. This story, with fine detail adapted for the relevant era, could have happened at any time and in many places.

There is no principal of leading and managing people advocated here that I have not seen succeeding in practise. Whenever leader/managers begin to employ these skills for the first time, they inevitably see positive changes in the behaviour of those around them.

The story does not present you with an exhaustive summary of each of the people management skills covered; instead it gives you enough to begin a journey of change. It is for you to take responsibility for that journey.

Ordinary People

But can you do it? Can you make the changes that the story suggests?

It is sometimes the case that 'ordinary people' feel themselves unsuited to leading change when faced with examples of successful, high profile leaders. At some level a voice may be saying 'I couldn't be like that', and quietly the spirit capitulates. In truth, my experience in developing leader/managers suggests that most are ordinary people, but that ordinary people can and do excel. An 'ordinary person' possessing some fundamental attributes can employ the skills described in the story and become an effective leader for positive change. This begs the question: 'Is an exceptional person a quite different kind of person to the majority, or is this person an 'ordinary person' behaving exceptionally?' My experience says that many exceptional leaders are 'ordinary people' behaving exceptionally, and what makes them exceptional is their ability to get ordinary people to behave exceptionally! (This space is for you to stop and think about that).

They are exceptional because they are different to a majority of leader/managers who are unable to gain this kind of performance from their team members, simply because they have not learned the necessary skills.

People Potential

As the story aims to illustrate, in failing to achieve this, the leader/manager fails both themselves and those that they lead. Not that their people would necessarily know that they are being failed, after all you don't miss what you don't know exists. People most commonly have little idea of how much they are capable. If their achievements are little, so their self-belief declines and with it their recognition and understanding of their own potential.

An ordinary person can understand and apply these skills, and in so doing make themselves into an extraordinary person. That is why I urge you to be optimistic about the potential of people to change for the better and why, when you apply these skills where they have not been applied before, you commonly see green shoots of ability in what appeared previously to be a hopelessly barren human landscape.

Actions and Reactions

Newton's third law of motion states that 'every action has an equal and opposite reaction'. This law can also be applied to managing people. We might debate 'equal and opposite' but for every action by a leader/manager toward his/her people you can be sure that there will be a reaction. 'Action' might be an aggressive comment, an instance of giving feedback, a coaching session, a delegation, the giving of praise, a smile, a frown and so on. For every action there is a reaction and that is why activity precedes results, things happen because of what is done. Therefore the leader/manager who wishes to make a difference must decide what he/she will do differently.

People and Organisations

Of course people and their performance is not the only facet of an organisation's behaviour that will contribute to the outcome. Others include: finance (its sufficiency and control), product (or service) its supply and suitability to the market place, and changing external factors beyond the control of the organisation. But note that each of these is greatly dependant upon the performance of people. It is people that will monitor and aim to regulate and control the flow of finance through an organisation. Many issues around finance are dictated by the skills, judgement and integrity of those people. Perhaps it is the availability of funding over which people within the organisation may have least influence, but real life David and Goliath stories are numerous. The small player with fewer resources must look to smart strategy to take on the giant. Where does the smart strategy come from? An organisation that has exposed its hidden treasure, so that it is no longer hidden but is at that organisation's disposal, is rich indeed, and great ideas will flow in abundance. From those ideas will surge the activity that delivers great results.

The same thinking applies to the other areas of an organisation's focus. For example it is people who will control how a product or service responds to changing circumstances. If a successful product becomes unsuitable, then that occurs because the people within that organisation did not recognise or take seriously the changes in the market place, or did not have the ability or the ideas to respond to that change. This can be summarised as people not performing to their potential, and when that happens it must be seen as the responsibility of management. This is management failing to use the human resource at its disposal.

What about external factors beyond the control of the organisation? Shortage of stock through supplier collapse, business lost to an inspired competitor, a world event that triggers price increases in raw materials or flattens demand for your product or service, fire that destroys your premises. Under such circumstances it is not what happens that is of most importance but how the organisation reacts to what happens. What is it that dictates the way organisations react? It is, of course, the people who make up the organisation, and the bulk of those people's reaction will be determined by the behaviour of their leader/managers. What sets organisations apart in the circumstances of threatening external factors is: Who could most quickly come up with new ideas for operating that will avoid the problem, and who could most quickly put those ideas into practise.

There remain factors beyond the above that cannot be overcome by optimum people performance.

The first is having the wrong person for the job, someone whose aptitude or intellect is wrongly matched to the job role. This book does not deal with that subject, but it is clearly critical that organisations take care to approach the recruitment of new members using the effective wisdom and tools that are available in abundance.

The second is someone whose attitude or mental outlook is beyond the reach of the influential tools of the people manager. It is a substantial benefit to know that you are managing people in a way that will bring out the best in them, since should they still not respond you can let them go with confidence and without that haunting feeling of 'I could have done better with that person'. As a people manager, you are not required to be a counsellor, psychiatrist or social worker - just to manage people well so that they can perform to the best of their ability. Those people can then be effectively judged fit or unfit for purpose.

The third factor is when external events are so overwhelming that even the best performing teams cannot overcome them. In these circumstances the battle will be lost, but recovery afterwards will be rapid as people work together to build themselves a new future.

This all means that when organisations establish values and objectives, they make a significant error if they do not put management of people at the heart of what they create. It is the management and leadership of people that should always be the centre point of such values, since they enable just about everything else that an organisation may aspire to.

Build the skills illustrated in the story, experience the confidence that comes as you recognise changes taking place around you and be sure to quietly pat yourself on the back and say 'I made that happen'.

Postscript

Jo-Anne stopped waving, her arm fell to her side. The door silently closed and the orange glow was replaced once again by eternal white.

'That was nice,' said Jo-Anne.

'Yes, wasn't it,' replied The Room.

'It's a shame that more people don't learn those things before they get here,' said Jo-Anne.

'It's a knowledge that seems to be easily forgotten,' replied The Room. 'People marvel at great achievements in their history and speculate on how they could have happened. Then someone rediscovers the exciting truth,' said The Room, 'that whenever a group of people gather together a great potential is created, a treasure of immense value. Impressive achievements are possible for any who discover that treasure.'

The End

Some Principles

What follows are the assumptions and guiding principles that lie behind the story of Hidden Treasure.

- All humans have substantial potential.

- Most human beings have a tendency to underestimate their own potential and the potential of others.

- When people are gathered together to accomplish a common task then the potential of each of those individuals has the best chance of being realised.

- Groups of people working together as a team can achieve to a level that is significantly beyond what those people would achieve acting as individuals.

- Leaders can create teams if those leaders employ the correct skills and strategies.

- Any group of people can work together as a team. The most effective teams will be those where the member's natural talents and attitudes complement each other.

- To create a team, the leader must first ensure that the prevailing communication style amongst the team is assertive. Without this the other elements cannot exist.

- A leader must understand what the prospective team members will need from him/herself and learn how to provide those things. This is leadership.

- A leader can then achieve team working by fulfilling three further criteria:

(a) maintaining the skills and knowledge of all team members at a level that allows them to accomplish their individual roles to a high standard,
(b) ensuring that there are common and agreed working methods,
(c) keeping all team members motivated to perform to a high standard within the team.

Subject Index